FIREARMS
FOR PERSONAL
PROTECTION

ARMED
DEFENSE
FOR THE NEW
GUN OWNER

JOSEPH VON BENEDIKT

Published by

Gun Digest® Books, an imprint of
F+W, A Content + eCommerce Company
Krause Publications • 700 East State Street • Iola, WI 54990-0001
715-445-2214 • 888-457-2873
www.krausebooks.com

To order books or other products call toll-free 1-800-258-0929
or visit us online at www.gundigeststore.com

ISBN-13: 978-1-4402-3899-4
ISBN-10: 1-4402-3899-5

Cover Design by Dave Hauser
Designed by Tom Nelsen
Edited by Corrina Peterson

Printed in the United States of America

For Guthrie
Who taught me the value of a Glock

TABLE OF CONTENTS

ACKNOWLEDGMENTS

To my wife Jenna, who supported and encouraged me and who suffered cheerfully through my stamping and grouching when the stress of working a full-time position as a magazine writer and attempting at the same time to pen a book sent me out of my nut, and to my lovely little children, who allowed my bedtime presence and the clacking of my keyboard to lull them to sleep in lieu of bedtime stories: Thank you.

Also thanks to my twin brother Aram, who gave up his time and served as a model for many of the photos contained herein, and to the other patient friends who allowed me to put guns in their hands and take pictures.

And finally, thanks to the excellent editors at FW Media, who worked their magic and polished my manuscript into readable form.

INTRODUCTION:

EARNING COMPETENCE

I was 13 when I first carried a gun for personal protection. My twin brother and our 14-year-old buddy were heading into the Southern Utah desert for a week of cow-punching. Only a few days before, a hiker had found 21 cattle dead and dying, shot with a small-caliber rifle. Pregnant or with small calves, no less. It was later determined that one of the more radical environmental groups had hired a hit man—if someone that murders cows can be dignified with the term—to go in and kill the cattle.

Young we were, but there wasn't going to be any of that on our watch. Lever-action carbines slid into dusty saddle scabbards without drama or fanfare, and we rode 17 miles through desert gulches and towering red cliffs to the line shack, prodding the packhorse into a trot so as to make it by dark.

Southern Utah in the '80s was still undiscovered, for the most part, and though I didn't know it at the time, I grew up among the last traces of the American West. Little kids could buy .22 shells at the local gas station without raising anyone's eyebrows. Teenagers packed guns when camping or working in the backcountry. My father gave me a reproduction Single Action Army in .44-40 in my mid teens, and I've been carrying handguns, rifles, and short shotguns in one form or another ever since.

My philosophy regarding firearms for personal protection is founded in practical mastery, versatility, and the unconscious competence that only comes with time and frequent use. I don't believe that compressed tactical training—as in the many tactical classes so popular today—can match long acquaintance and familiarity with a firearm, though to be sure such training is a great way to attain a jump-start on correct handling techniques.

Unconscious competence, to my mind, will always trump pseudo-tactical enthusiasm. Such competence cannot be wooed, cannot be purchased; it must be earned.

Where do you start? With knowledge and practice. You'll never master a gun lying untouched on a shelf any more than you will a guitar gathering dust in the corner.

The knowledge is in this book and others like it. The practice, and the competence that follows, that's up to you.

This book may be read cohesively or sporadically. Start at the front and read right through to the back page, or start in the middle and dip here and there as interest dictates. Each chapter complements the others yet stands on its own.

CHAPTER 1

SEMIAUTOMATIC VS. REVOLVER

Some time ago, my schoolteacher nephew and I headed out of town and pulled off the highway onto a two-track in likely-looking coyote country. Utah's bounty was up, and both of us figured we could use a few extra bucks. I removed my Smith & Wesson M&P9 Shield from my waistband, stuck it into my war bag, and climbed into my camo clothing. As I belted on my revolver—a customized Taurus 425—I noticed that my nephew had removed his Beretta Nano and was threading a holstered Ruger SP101 onto his belt. I had to laugh. It was the perfect demonstration of the fact that sometimes revolvers are more suitable than semiautos, and vice versa.

Semiautomatic handguns are typically the better choice for suburban and in-home use and, when cared for and kept clean, are the flavor of the day in what I'll term combat zones—whether an Afghanistan outpost, a disaster area overrun by consequence-free crime, or an apocalyptic end-of-days scenario.

Revolvers and semiautomatics are very different beasts, though both are capable personal protection arms. Know the differences and choose what best fits your environment and needs.

Revolvers are less susceptible to dirty, adverse conditions than are semiautos. If your time is spent in the outdoors, and you prefer a low-maintenance approach to your gear, you're likely best served with a revolver.

Revolvers, on the other hand, are the better option when sand, dust, and involuntary neglect add up to an environment that may challenge a semiauto's reliability. They are just more reliable in very dirty conditions. Also, revolvers tend to be chambered for more powerful cartridges—sometimes much more powerful—than semiautos. While this is an advantage in the backcountry or around livestock and heavy predators, it's a disadvantage in an urban neighborhood composed of thin walls and sleeping children.

Can the two vastly different handgun types cross over in usefulness? Absolutely. However, each has its strengths and weaknesses. Here's a look at the defining characteristics of each type.

REVOLVERS

Since revolvers don't depend on harnessing the energy of a cartridge to function, like semiautos do, there's just one less thing to go wrong. Squib loads, dud primers, a tight cartridge too stubborn to chamber easily—none of these affect revolvers. Additionally, since human muscle works a revolver's action, bits of sand, lint, dust, or fouling that would choke a semiauto can be overcome by, well, a little more muscle. Just ear that hammer back and let fly.

Revolvers have the virtue of extreme simplicity. The double-action versions best for personal protection may be fired by simply pulling the trigger through it's long stroke, which rotates the cylinder to a fresh cartridge, cocks the hammer, and then drops the hammer and fires the gun.

With practice, a revolver can be reloaded quickly via the use of a Speedloader.

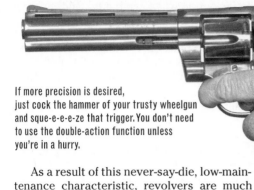

If more precision is desired, just cock the hammer of your trusty wheelgun and sque-e-e-e-ze that trigger. You don't need to use the double-action function unless you're in a hurry.

As a result of this never-say-die, low-maintenance characteristic, revolvers are much favored by outdoorsmen and country folks.

As mentioned earlier, the magnum cartridges frequently chambered in revolvers can offer quite an advantage for rural use, too. They provide more downrange reach, more downrange energy, and typically a great deal more penetration—important when scraping an enterprising black bear out of the bacon griddle next to your tent, or trying to kill a wigged-out saddle horse that's running like a banshee while you bounce along the cactus-covered ground with your boot stuck in the stirrup.

> *Your revolver will never turn into a one-shooter because you misplace your magazines.*

Revolvers are slower to reload. With practice and a good speedloader (a device that holds the bases of a cylinder-worth of cartridges, and drops them into the open cylinder of a double-action revolver at the twist of a knob) or moon clip (a spring steel device that holds a cylinder-full of cartridges, and goes into and out of the gun with them), a good revolver man can get back into action pretty quickly. But, speedloaders and moon clips are awkward to carry, and it takes good training to achieve speed and surety. Single-action revolvers are even slower. Much slower.

On the plus side, your revolver will never turn into a one-shooter because you misplace your magazines. And if you've got a little survivalist in your nature, you'll appreciate the fact that empty cartridge brass is easy to collect—just dump it into your pocket after eject-

As demonstrated by this .44 Magnum beside a 9mm cartridge, revolvers are often far more powerful than semiautos—a good thing in rural areas but not so good in crowded urban areas where overpenetration is a bad thing. On the other hand, most semiautos hold more ammo—sometimes lots more—and recoil less, making for faster follow-up shots.

Some revolvers are cut for moon clips such as those shown here. With practice a good shooter can reload as quickly as a semiauto shooter. But moon clips are awkward to carry.

ing it. With care, you'll never loose a piece, and you never have to hunt for little sparkly brass bits flung indiscriminately away by your greedy semiauto.

Revolvers are either single action or double action. Single actions are the archetypical western sidearm. Nothing surpasses them for panache, and with practice they become quite serviceable personal protection guns. However, they're slow to reload, and the hammer must be manually cocked prior to each shot.

I love single actions, but for the purpose of this book they are just not as suitable for personal protection use, and we'll leave it at that and move on to double-action guns.

Double-action handguns can be fired by simply pulling the trigger. The long, sweeping pull will cock the hammer rearward, rotate the cylinder so a fresh cartridge is in place, and then drop the hammer at the end of its stroke, firing the revolver. Old-timers called them "self-cockers," which was a pretty apt term.

If more precision is desired, a double-action revolvers can be cocked manually and then fired by squeezing the trigger, just like a single-action. Single-action function has the virtue of a clean, crisp, creep-free trigger pull, making careful, accurate shots easier.

Revolvers have the appealing virtue of simplicity. Neophyte shooters intuitively grasp how they function, and the lack of slides, slide stops, magazine releases, decockers, and safeties of various flavors is attractive. Many women opt to carry a compact revolver for that winsome simplicity, frequently compounded by the fact that petite women sometimes struggle to pull back a semiauto pistol's slide in order to chamber a cartridge.

As I see it, the revolver has only a few drawbacks as a prime personal protection sidearm. They have limited capacity, they are slow to reload, and the cartridges for which they are chambered are often overpowered for city and in-home use.

The first two drawbacks are what they are, and shooters opting for a revolver should plan on spending time practicing reloading in order to even the odds a bit. The over-power issue, on the other hand, can be turned to the owner's benefit by choosing ammunition with hollow-point projectiles designed for dramatic expansion, in a light-for-caliber weight. The affect is two-fold: with less mass, projectiles will penetrate less, and the large on-impact expansion will slow bullets down, dumping more energy into the bad guy and reducing the chance of a pass-through that could potentially endanger family members or neighbors.

It boils down to this: with the correct ammunition and some quality practice-time manipulating the gun, a revolver will do anything you'll ever need it to.

SEMIAUTOMATICS

As far and away the most popular type of sidearm for personal protection, the semiauto's primary attractions are high capacity and excellent rapid-fire capability. With correct maintenance and quality ammunition, good semiautos are very reliable, too.

I grew up carrying a revolver while working cattle in Southwestern desert country. None of the guys I knew owned a semiauto, because prevailing opinion was that they couldn't cut the mustard in the country and conditions in which we worked. I've since learned differently—a good semiauto can take an awful lot of abuse and still function reliably.

When I first started carrying a semiauto (a Colt Gold Cup 1911 in .45 ACP) it wasn't for high capacity, it was for the rapid-fire characteristic. The Colt didn't really offer much in the way of additional round count—my surplus G.I. magazines were seven-rounders. Heck, my single-action .44-40s held six. But I couldn't shoot a single-action as quickly as a semiauto, and though I could hose rounds downrange pretty quickly out of a double-action, I couldn't shoot it fast nearly as accurately as my 1911.

Speed is one of the most important advantages that a semiauto offers the average person. Sure, there are revolver shooters who can shoot faster and more accurately than 99 percent of the semiauto shooters out there, but the reality is that, for most folks, semiautos are a little easier to shoot fast than revolvers.

Semiautos are often the best choice for personal and home protection. Just be sure you get one you can operate comfortably—many shooters with low hand strength struggle to function the slide of a big semiauto, especially under stress.

One of the biggest—if not the biggest—appeal of the modern semiauto is very high capacity. Most polymer-frame 9mms hold from 15 to 19 rounds in the magazine.

> *There are a lot of situations in which it would be mighty comforting to have 50-plus rounds available.*

Throw in high capacity, and you've got a very supportable argument that the semiauto makes a better personal protection gun than does a revolver. Truth is, most of today's popular designs hold more cartridges than a wheelgun—usually a lot more. Even a modern magazine in a .45-caliber 1911 holds eight rounds, plus one in the chamber. That's a total of nine, for a 50-percent increase on the capacity of most revolvers. Throw in high-capacity guns, such as Glock's G17, Smith & Wesson's M&P9, and Springfield's XD(m), all of which contain 17+1 to 19+1 rounds in the magazine, and you've got three times the capacity of a revolver. Three times! Add a couple of easy-to-carry magazines in innocent-looking belt sheaths, and you can comfortably carry over 50 rounds on your person.

You can argue that, in most of today's typical defensive encounters, you shouldn't need even a tenth that number. You'd be right. However, what about that non-typical encounter? Or—admit it, we all think about it—an end-of-days scenario? There are a lot of situations in which it would be mighty comforting to have 50-plus rounds available.

Semiautos do have some drawbacks. They are clean freaks. They are also picky about subpar ammo. Whereas a revolver will accept anything that fits properly into a cylinder chamber and will dutifully fire it downrange, a semiauto must have cartridges with the correct bullet nose geometry for reliable feeding, enough propellant to fully function the slide but not so much that it batters the internal mechanics, correct case length for proper headspacing... all this within spec so that it flows into the chamber and out again without hanging up in a gun powered purely by energy harnessed from the explosion of the cartridge itself. Looked at from an informed, objective position, that's a lot to ask. It's a marvel than so many semiautos are the reliability champs that they are.

The magazine is a semiauto's Achilles tendon. With a cheap, faulty, or damaged magazine (note the dented feed lip) reliability goes to pot.

Most semiautos are clean freaks. Treat them with care, and they will always take care of you.

The very magazines that provide high-capacity firepower can—if lost or damaged—cripple a semiauto and, in essence, turn it into a single-shot. Or worse, incapacitate it completely if it's one of the models with a magazine disconnect safety that prevents it from firing unless a magazine is inserted. These days, we take magazines pretty lightly, as most of us have a spare or several. But in the early days of semiautos, folks considered the potential more gravely. Many early models—especially those of European design—didn't allow magazines to fall freely when released; this influence extended up through the first-generation Glocks.

Limited energy and penetration are another characteristic of shots fired from most semi-auto handguns. In many scenarios, limited penetration is an advantage. A 9mm hollow-point projectile is much less likely to penetrate through walls than a classic soft-point .357 Magnum projectile. But it does limit a semiauto's suitability for certain tasks. I know of two Alaskan bear guides who carry semiauto .45 ACP pistols for backup. What tomfoolery. Even the more powerful revolver calibers (until you get to the obscenely powerful .500 S&W Magnum) are unsuitable for stopping a bear with uncivilized intentions, let alone a semiauto with very limited penetration and (in bear terms) not nearly enough energy on impact.

However, we're discussing personal protection firearms here, and none of the above semiauto drawbacks really apply. Shoot quality ammunition, and purchase plenty of magazines and keep track of them diligently. As long as you attend to those two details, a good semiauto makes more sense than a revolver most of the time.

High capacity coupled with ammo that is light in weight mounts a convincing argument in favor of today's modern, light, low-recoil semiautos. These three Glock G17 magazines total over 50 rounds of 9mm ammo.

CHAPTER 2

CALIBER CHOICES

Any discussion of cartridge suitability is a delightfully perilous undertaking. Cartridges engender loyalty and dislike as effectively as do in-laws, and shooters will defend favorites with pugnacious aggression or tramp those regarded with disdain into the mud with glee.

I'm bound to hurt some feelings here, but for the purposes of this book, I'm going to smugly ignore all the fantastic but generally unnecessary cartridges such as the .45 GAP, .357 SIG, and 10mm S&W. Yes, they all perform well in their sphere, and some offer performance that rightly should be trumpeted to the skies, but as a matter of wallet-flattening fact, they are too obscure, too expensive, too hard for average handgunners to shoot well, or all of the above. The cartridges suggested and detailed here are veteran performers that earned inclusion through proven history and common availability.

Cartridges for semiautomatic pistols and for revolvers are two very different breeds. Aside from the obvious differences, such as velocity and energy, there are differences in functional characteristics. For example, most revolver cartridges are rimmed, meaning that there's a rim or lip around the base of the cartridge, which the cartridge headspaces on, preventing the cartridge from entering the chamber too deeply. In double-action revolvers, the rim also enables the extractor to remove cartridges from the cylinder.

Typically, revolver cases are bigger, longer, and have rims on their bases. Semiauto cartridges, on the other hand, tend to be compact and have rimless bases (sometimes also called rebated rims). Shown left to right: 9mm Luger, .45 ACP, .44 Magnum, .357 Magnum.

Most revolver cartridges headspace (position) off of the rim, as shown by the .44 Magnums in the cylinder of this classic Smith & Wesson Model 29.

Many obscure cartridges, such as those shown here, offer the performance to be excellent personal protection rounds, but limited availability removes them from popular contention. Shown left to right: .45 GAP, 10mm Auto, .357 SIG.

The smooth, parallel sides of good semiauto cartridges allow easy feeding from magazines and into chambers. Note the absence of a rim.

Most semiauto cartridges, on the other hand, are not rimmed. Rims complicated feeding from a magazine stacked sardine-full of cartridges. Most semiauto cartridges headspace on the mouth of the case, making case length of vital importance. If it's a bit short, and the cartridge falls a bit too far into the chamber, two things can happen: the primer can be slightly out of reach of the firing pin, resulting in a dud, or if the cartridge does fire, the excess room in the chamber can cause a pressure spike when the cartridge detonates and the case shifts rearward in the chamber. Trimming cases to correct length is very important when reloading semiauto ammunition.

This star-studded cartridge lineup reads like a who's who in the world of self-defense cartridges: From left: .380 Auto, 9mm Luger, .40 S&W, .45 ACP, .38 Special, .357 Magnum, and the low-versatility daddy of them all: the .44 Magnum.

Although myriad cartridges exist for both firearm types, there are only a few that I consider really suitable for widespread recommendation for personal defense. That's not to say that others aren't just as accurate, or powerful, or reliable, or effective. The cartridges discussed in this chapter have earned the right to be included. They are capable in terms of power, accuracy, and reliability, and they are commonly available in both terms of ammunition itself and in guns chambered for the cartridge.

Here, listed from lightest to heaviest, are the cartridges that history has proven most successful, and that I can personally recommend without qualm. Let's start with revolver cartridges.

REVOLVER CARTRIDGES

.38 SPECIAL

This cartridge isn't known as a stopper of frothing-at-the-mouth goliaths. It doesn't hit particularly hard. However, it's like the minivan of revolver cartridges; though unglamorous, few things are more versatile, useful, and forgiving.

> *The .38 Special is like the minivan of revolver cartridges; though unglamorous, few things are more versatile, useful, and forgiving.*

Police revolvers for decades were chambered for either .38 Special or .357 Magnum. Since the .357 Magnum is simply a lengthened, higher-pressure version of it's parent .38, and since revolver cartridges headspace on the rim rather than the case mouth, the older, shorter .38 may safely be fired in the chambers of a .357 Magnum handgun.

While it isn't Jack the Giant Killer, the .38 Special is nothing to sneeze at. In modern, hollow-point guise (shown at right), especially in high-pressure +P loads, it's a reasonably good self-defense round. Lawmen carried pedestrian round-nose lead-bullet loads (remember the single cartridge Barney Fife carried in his shirt pocket) such as the cartridge shown at left for decades, but they had limited stopping efficiency.

While not as effective on impact as the magnum, the .38 Special is much friendlier to shoot. Many magnum-issued cops chose to practice with and sometimes even carry .38s rather than the full-bore magnum hammers, and many police departments issued .38 cartridges even if their officers had .357 Magnum handguns.

Like the 9mm Luger semiauto cartridge, modern projectiles elevate the impact performance of the .38 Special significantly, especially in +P (high pressure) loads. Original .38 police ammo was generally loaded with cast lead, round-nose bullets at very modest velocities. As you can imagine, they didn't exactly knock a bad guy into the nearest horse-watering trough.

Current high-performance defense loads feature projectiles that range from 110 grains at around 1,010 fps up to 158-grains at some 800 fps providing around 150 to 200 foot-pounds of energy. I tend to choose bullets on the lighter side when carrying a .38 Special, for two reasons: the higher velocity provides more predictable bullet expansion on impact, and the lighter bullets tend to penetrate less, minimizing the likelihood of semi-spent bullets steaming through the neighbor's bedroom.

One of the best of the modern lot is Hornady's 110-grain Critical Defense load. It shoots a good hollow-point projectile with a squishy rubbery plastic tip, which prevents failure of the hollow point to expand by keeping heavy clothing or whatnot from plugging the hollow point. In essence, on impact the squishy substance acts hydraulically, forcing the hollow point to expand immediately and dramatically. Other favorites include Speer's 135-grain Gold Dot load, Winchester's 130-grain PDX1 +P load, and Remington's 125-grain HD +P load.

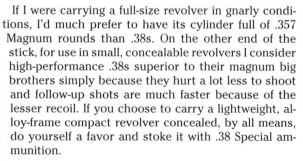

Undoubtedly the most versatile revolver chambering in existence, partly due to its ability to safely chamber and shoot .38 Special ammo, the .357 Magnum is powerful and deadly while still easy to shoot in a full-size handgun. It gets a little peppy in compact guns.

If I were carrying a full-size revolver in gnarly conditions, I'd much prefer to have its cylinder full of .357 Magnum rounds than .38s. On the other end of the stick, for use in small, concealable revolvers I consider high-performance .38s superior to their magnum big brothers simply because they hurt a lot less to shoot and follow-up shots are much faster because of the lesser recoil. If you choose to carry a lightweight, alloy-frame compact revolver concealed, by all means, do yourself a favor and stoke it with .38 Special ammunition.

■ .357 MAGNUM

If the .38 Special is the minivan of revolver cartridges, the .357 Magnum is the 4x4 pickup truck. Loud, hard-hitting, and very authoritative on the receiving end, it is without doubt the most capable, versatile revolver cartridge for personal protection.

> *If the .38 Special is the minivan of revolver cartridges, the .357 Magnum is the 4x4 pickup truck.*

Why? Because it achieves tremendous performance without generating too much recoil for the average shooter to handle—when fired in a full-size revolver. (In my opinion, unless you are a very accomplished shooter impervious to recoil, .357 Magnums have little place in compact, lightweight, concealable revolvers—that's the realm of high-performance .38 Specials.)

Speaking of the venerable .38 Special, it may—as mentioned in the section on it—be fired in .357 Magnum revolvers, adding versatility to revolvers chambered for the .357, and making for much more pleasant practice and plinking.

Many early .357 Magnum loads featured hard-cast lead bullets, and in some cases, they weren't hard enough to handle the aggressive pressures and high velocities generated by the cartridge. As a result, they tended to "lead" barrels badly—in essence leaving smears of lead in the rifling grooves, which eventually built up to the point that accuracy didn't just deteriorate, it went away completely.

Eventually ammo manufacturers moved away from all but the occasional mild cast-lead .357 Magnum loads, instead loading jacketed soft point bullets that didn't lead up rifling and offered better expansion characteristics anyway.

Common bullet weights range from 125 grains at around 1,500 fps, up to 158 grains pushing 1,250 fps; providing energy between 550 to 630 foot-pounds at the muzzle—pretty potent. You can also find the odd heavier 170- or 180-grain load, which work pretty well for deer hunting.

The heavier jacketed projectiles penetrate very well. Depending on the shooter's environment, that can be an advantage or a potential danger. The last thing you want are bullets passing through an attacker and endangering innocent people. For personal protection around the house or in urban areas, a fast 125-grain hollow-point bullet is best, as it will expand dramatically on impact, imparting a lot of shock to a violent attacker yet minimizing penetration. I reserve the heavier 158-grain and similar bullets for use when I anticipate the need for deep penetration.

As a matter of revolver-favoring fact, the .357 Magnum hits with more energy than any of the popular semiauto cartridges, including the legendary .45 ACP. Yet a revolver chambered for it can be turned into a mild-mannered pussycat simply by loading it with .38 Special cartridges. Without doubt it is the most versatile, adaptable, capable chambering available for a personal protection revolver.

Dramatically overpowered for personal protection use anywhere but in rural and backcountry areas, where livestock and wildlife can pose a threat, the .44 Magnum is the quintessential big-bore revolver cartridge. Practical use in urban environments is limited because of overpenetration issues that endanger neighbors.

▉ .44 MAGNUM

This cartridge doesn't even belong in this "recommended" section. Not that it isn't capable—rather, it's as over-qualified as a cartridge can get in the capability department.

It's just that few folks can handle the brutal recoil generated by blasting a 240-grain bullet downrange at 1,350 fps. I'm including it because, well, I can't not include it. It's the third-most popular revolver cartridge in America, and far and away the most powerful of the top three.

Properly developed for hunting and for use when a wheel-less hand cannon is called for, the .44 Magnum earned legendary status in the hands of television's 1980's tough-cop character Dirty Harry—Clint Eastwood played the part, toting a Smith & Wesson Model 29, and bad guys shot with it levitated and crashed backward through doors. Like most Hollywood characterizations of bullet impact effects, that's rather optimistic—bullets from the .44 Magnum hit hard, very hard, and expand well, but they won't pick up a character of nefarious bent and catapult him into the nearest corner.

You'll get neither fast follow-up shots nor controllable recoil with the .44 Magnum. What you'll get is a cartridge that will shoot through most barriers, such as car doors, typical walls, and so on; that is very good (as handgun cartridges go) for big game hunting; and that puts big holes in whatever it hits. For protection against bear, or use around big, aggressive livestock, it makes a lot of sense.

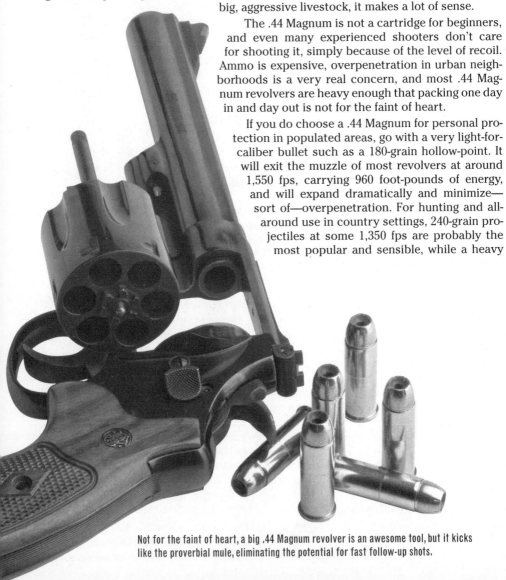

The .44 Magnum is not a cartridge for beginners, and even many experienced shooters don't care for shooting it, simply because of the level of recoil. Ammo is expensive, overpenetration in urban neighborhoods is a very real concern, and most .44 Magnum revolvers are heavy enough that packing one day in and day out is not for the faint of heart.

If you do choose a .44 Magnum for personal protection in populated areas, go with a very light-for-caliber bullet such as a 180-grain hollow-point. It will exit the muzzle of most revolvers at around 1,550 fps, carrying 960 foot-pounds of energy, and will expand dramatically and minimize—sort of—overpenetration. For hunting and all-around use in country settings, 240-grain projectiles at some 1,350 fps are probably the most popular and sensible, while a heavy

Not for the faint of heart, a big .44 Magnum revolver is an awesome tool, but it kicks like the proverbial mule, eliminating the potential for fast follow-up shots.

300-grain projectile at 1,150 fps penetrates wonderfully and makes a great hunting bullet. Energy ranges from 850 foot pounds up to an impressive 960 foot-pounds.

There are more powerful handgun cartridges, but none that are commonly available, and all of them come in a gun that is big enough to pound steel fence posts into rocky soil. They are brutality incarnate and so loud that in reality no hearing protection is sufficient to fully avoid hearing damage.

I love the .44 Magnum cartridge—it excels within its sphere, and is popular enough that ammo is plentiful, but in reality, it just isn't a very good choice for personal protection due to limited versatility.

SEMIAUTO CARTRIDGES

▨ .380 AUTO

I know, I know. James Bond used a .32 Auto, and every bad guy he shot at tipped over like a domino. But in the real world, even the slightly bigger .380 is a marginal personal-protection cartridge, and it has achieved suitable status courtesy only of high-tech projectiles of recent design that have drastically improved its lethality.

Frankly, in terms of usefulness the .380 is limited to con-

cealed-carry guns. While it's got great characteristics that make it a perfect candidate for deep carry in a tailored business suit, or light summer wear, or for carry by petite women that don't want their handgun interfering with their sense of style, it just doesn't have enough poop to make it interesting in a full-size, high-capacity handgun. It shoots a projectile of the same diameter as the 9mm, but not with nearly the velocity, nor with as much weight. While the 9mm, with good ammo, crosses over into the territory of really effective fighting cartridges, the .380 does not.

The tiny .380 Auto squeaks onto the suitable-for-protection list—barely—courtesy of its ability to fit into very small concealable semiautos. It's projectile is the same diameter as that of the 9mm, just lighter and travelling slower so it has less authority on impact. For a deep-concealment gun, it's just perfect.

Common bullet weights hover pretty consistently around 90 to 95 grains, rated at an optimistic 980 to 1,000 feet per second (fps) in terms of velocity. That gives the .380 around 200 foot-pounds of energy at the muzzle, with a very light bullet. Contrast that with the 9mm, which offers 325 to 370 foot-pounds of energy, or to a legendary man-stopper such as the .45 ACP, with average energy from 390 to 490 foot pounds, and you can understand why I consider it marginal.

On the plus side, it's small enough and short enough that it fits beautifully into magazines suitable for the very small grips of honest-to-goodness pocket pistols. It has enough frontal diameter and just enough bullet weight to impart fairly reasonable shock upon impact, assuming that quality hollow point bullets are used (avoid using full-metal-jacket (FMJ) projectiles for defensive purposes). And finally, recoil is quite mild, making it as pleasant to shoot in a tiny handgun as an adequate cartridge can possibly be.

▨ 9MM LUGER

More than one WWII veteran has told me that even German officers preferred the Colt .45-caliber 1911s that the Americans had, and given the opportunity would jump at the chance to clandestinely obtain a .45 and carry it in preference to their 9mm Luger. Wartime legend has it that the .45 was as good an enemy-stopper as the 9mm was bad.

So why is it included here? Because it's one of the finest self-defense cartridges available.

> *The 9mm, with current, high-performance expanding-bullet loads, hits hard enough to play with the big dogs.*

Arguably the most popular handgun cartridge in the world, the 9mm is very effective as a self-defense cartridge provided it's loaded with modern, expanding hollow-points. However, when loaded with sleek full metal jacketed (FMJ) projectiles as shown at right, it not nearly as effective.

Lest I leave you scratching your head in puzzlement, let me qualify that. Current, high-performance 9mm ammunition makes it one of the finest self-defense cartridges available. Wartime ammunition utilized full metal jacketed (FMJ) bullets, both in 9mm and .45. While .45 FMJ bullets are large in diameter and have quite a blunt nose profile, 9mm FMJ bullets are slender, sleek, and somewhat pointy. Impact differences between the two are dramatic. In essence, .45 FMJ bullets make a big hole and impart a lot of shock on impact, while 9mm FMJ bullets tend to pencil through without dumping much energy. An adrenaline-filled bad guy could soak up several hits from your 9mm and still come over and stick his bayonet in you. Bad.

The big, huge, major elevating factor in making the 9mm a good man-stopper is advanced bullet technology. Design a hollow-point 9mm projectile to expand to significantly greater diameter than a FMJ .45, combine that with the high velocity generated by the 9mm cartridge, and you've got a genuine knock-down fighting cartridge.

Most ammo companies now offer advanced expanding bullets in the 9mm. Some of the best are found in Hornady's Critical Duty and Critical Defense lines, Winchester's PDX1, Speer's Gold Dot, and Remington's HD ammo. The best of them will pass the FBI protocol tests (an advanced series of tests including shooting into ballistic gel through heavy clothing, auto windshield glass, multiple layers of sheet metal, and so on, demand-

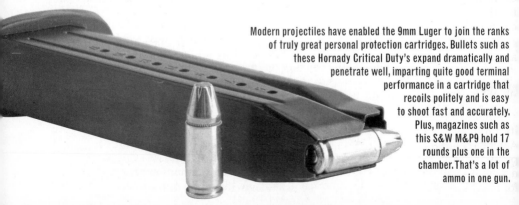

Modern projectiles have enabled the 9mm Luger to join the ranks of truly great personal protection cartridges. Bullets such as these Hornady Critical Duty's expand dramatically and penetrate well, imparting quite good terminal performance in a cartridge that recoils politely and is easy to shoot fast and accurately. Plus, magazines such as this S&W M&P9 hold 17 rounds plus one in the chamber. That's a lot of ammo in one gun.

ing consistent bullet expansion and exceeding a minimum penetration criteria throughout), but all perform pretty well.

Common bullet weights range from 115 grains at 1,180 fps to 147 grains at 1,000 fps, generating from 325 up to 370 foot pounds of energy.

If you choose a handgun chambered in 9mm Luger, keep your magazines loaded with the best premium expanding-bullet loads that you can afford. Practice with cheaper same-weight FMJ loads, but don't depend on them to stop an intruder before he can hit you over the head with his tire iron.

The 9mm, with current, high-performance expanding-bullet loads, hits hard enough to play with the big dogs. That accepted, it must be admitted that it's three other great virtues—high capacity, low recoil, and worldwide availability—elevate it to a position among the very finest personal protection cartridges available today.

■ .40 S&W

Frankly, I'm not a big fan of the .40 S&W. In my less-than-humble opinion, it tries to achieve high capacity in the spirit of the 9mm, and the impact authority of the .45, and ends up being a loud, blasty, sharp-recoiling hybrid that is less than either. That said, there are enough very knowledgeable shooters that respect the .40 S&W greatly that I must grudgingly admit that I'm likely not entirely justified in my personal indifference to the cartridge.

A stunted sibling of the excellent but hard-kicking, almost-obsolete 10mm Auto, the .40 S&W was created in an effort to increase the authority of high-capacity pistols. Widely used by law enforcement personnel across the country, it shoots a bullet that is a little larger in diameter and a little heavier than the 9mm, plus almost as fast as the 9mm. Actual recoil is measurably less than that generated by a .45; however, it is sharper due to the fairly high muzzle velocity, making perceived differences in recoil negligible. In fact, many shooters claim to prefer the big push of the .45 to the sharp slam of the .40.

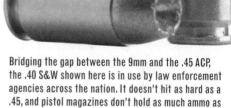

Bridging the gap between the 9mm and the .45 ACP, the .40 S&W shown here is in use by law enforcement agencies across the nation. It doesn't hit as hard as a .45, and pistol magazines don't hold as much ammo as those in 9mm, but it's a good hybrid between the two.

Common bullet weights range from 155 grains at 1,160 fps to 180 grains at 1,000 fps, generating 360 to 460 foot-pounds of energy.

One advantage of the .40 S&W is that, in times of ammo shortage such as we've seen after the recent elections, 9mm ammo can be downright hard to find, while a few boxes of .40 S&W, not being quite as popular, may still lurk on gun shop shelves. On the other hand, in really bad times it will probably be easier to scrounge or barter for 9mm—because of that same popularity—than for .40 S&W.

If you like the .40 S&W, by all means, use it. It's nationally popular, it performs well, and is quite widely available.

■ .45 ACP

Ahhh… the great .45. History, panache, and class mingle with unquestioned authority. Probably the greatest combat handgun cartridge of all time, the .45 has fought beside America's servicemen through every war since the Great War. In the 1980s it was replaced by the 9mm-chambered Beretta M9 in most branches of the service, but the Navy maintained the 1911 .45, and so it soldiers on. My guess is that it will continue to do so for many a decade.

Over the past century the .45 ACP/1911 pistol combination has become the most proven combat handgun combination in history.

Here's the reason that the legendary .45 ACP became, well, legendary during the World Wars. Conventions of war demand an FMJ bullet, and the broad, blunt nose of the .45 hits hard. Much harder than the pointy, smaller 9mm FMJ at left.

As mentioned in the discussion of the 9mm Luger, military full metal jacket (FMJ) bullets for the .45 are big, blunt, and hit like an Irish tracklayer's sledgehammer. Modern hollow-points of advanced design hit even harder, expanding dramatically—sometimes as large as an inch in diameter—and imparting tremendously effective stopping power.

Though .45 ACP ammunition is significantly more expensive than 9mm or .40, it has one great unsung virtue—even lowly FMJ practice ammunition is pretty effective in a deadly altercation. Neither the 9mm or .40 can claim that. I carry the best defense ammunition I can afford in the magazines of my .45s, but if I ran out and all I had was a quantity of FMJ stuff that I'd purchased for practicing with, I'd use it and be confident in it.

Average projectile weights run from about 185 grains at 970 fps up to 230 grains at 850 to 950 in high-pressure +P loads, generating from 390 to 490 foot-pounds of energy. Not only is that a substantial amount more energy than the 9mm offers, but just as importantly, the .45s larger frontal diameter causes considerably more bad-guy-stopping trauma.

Like all cartridges, it has a few drawbacks. Ammo is more expensive than either 9mm or .40 S&W. Recoil is substantial; inexperienced shooters are much more likely to develop an uncontrollable flinch from shooting a .45 than if they were armed with a 9mm. Magazine capacity is usually limited to seven or eight rounds, and the high-capacity .45 ACPs that do exist tend to be uncomfortably bulky in the grip.

Arguably the single best fighting handgun cartridge ever invented, the historic .45 ACP is legendary for its effectiveness, even with non-expanding FMJ bullets.

Together, the 1911 pistol and the .45 ACP cartridge became the most proven combat handgun combination in history. It's the perfect synthesis of ideal fighting cartridge in a handgun of mechanical genius. Separated, each is still extraordinary, but the unrivaled union of the two has probably defended more American lives—soldier and citizen—than any other handgun/cartridge in history.

CHAPTER 3

CONCEALED-CARRY VS. NIGHTSTAND GUNS

Purebred concealed-carry handguns are a class of their own. You might say that they have superlative social skills—they fit in anywhere without causing ruffled feathers, courtesy of their ability to blend in. The real McCoy fits in your hand or a small pocket perfectly, points like your index finger, fires no matter how much belly button lint is in its mechanism, and makes you want to say "Bond, James Bond."

Good "nightstand" guns are capable fighting handguns—they have no need to be subtle or have finesse in anything but efficiently stopping whatever is threatening your life. Usually, big, powerful, and/or high capacity handguns best fit the job.

Top concealed-carry handguns are sophisticated enough to disappear with a minimum of effort, yet—if carried properly—be readily available.

While big handguns can be concealed, it's a much harder than hiding a small, flat gun designed for the purpose. Note how the grip of this Glock G17 "prints" through this tee shirt.

Although both of these semiautos are made by Smith & Wesson and chambered in 9mm, they are very different beasts. One makes a priority of being easy to shoot fast and accurately and offer a ton of ammo; the other's job is to disappear like an unwanted relative yet be reliable when called upon. One is what I term a nightstand gun—best for everything except hiding. The other is a perfect concealed companion—you forget it's there until you need it.

"Nightstand" guns, on the other hand, have no need to be subtle. They can be as subtle as Bond's buddy "Jaws" and serve their purpose admirably. All about getting the job done in the most dicey situations, when slippery with fear-sweat and controlled through a fog of hastily-departed slumber, an honest nightstand gun is hand-filling, is high capacity, is fitted with a light of villain-blinding strength, and performs admirably when operated with gross motor skills.

Contrary to the laws of physics, all too many gun owners desire one handgun to fill both missions.

I'll concede that in a pinch it can be done. If it must be done, one is better off pressing a concealed-carry handgun into bedside guard duty than the other way around. Why? For the simple reason that it's pretty hard to disguise a Glock 21 or it's beefy ilk under a tee shirt, golf sweater, sport coat, or anything short of a bomber jacket. Yet in a pinch a flat, diminutive pocket gun can accompany you on a quest to confront a bump in the night.

Short of an apocalyptic scene, when you'd want about three little hideout guns seques-tered about your person and a

We want our guns to be small, yet powerful and easy to shoot. Pretty tall order, but good ones such as this Smith & Wesson M&P9 Shield accomplish it.

big, powerfully bad high-capacity pistol hung on your hip in an immediately accessible position, these two handgun types (carry and nightstand guns) are the two most practi-cal, useful, and likely to be called into action of all personal protection arms.

That being the case, let's take a close look at the vastly different demands placed on each type, and the characteristics that allow each to excel. (And yes, we'll discuss guns for apocalyptic conditions in a later chapter.)

CONCEALED-CARRY HANDGUNS

Gun owners tend to get positively high maintenance about concealed-carry guns. For good reason, too. We want them to disappear into our pocket (or waistband, or ankle, or armpit), yet leap into our hand without hanging up or snagging on the way to greet a bad guy. We want them to be small enough to disappear like the Ace of Spades up a gamblers' sleeve, yet be polite in recoil. We want them to point naturally, shoot reliably and accurate-ly, and hit iniquitous characters like a battleaxe. And dammit, we want them to look good.

Flatness is one of the great defining characteristics of a good concealed-carry handgun. Note that this Smith & Wesson M&P9 Shield is less than an inch in width—the 9mm cartridge standing by it is longer than that.

In short, they're expected to accompany us like a sophisticated date and protect us like a country lawyer.

That's a lot to lay on a petite gun. Small mechanisms are not always robust, and physics place increased demands on operating systems. Fat cartridges tend to be sluggish between magazine and chamber, and curtailed slide travel must squeeze those fat cartridges up minimum-space feed ramps.

Small, flat, controllable, powerful, reliable, accurate, and aesthetic. The incredible thing is that not only are there guns that achieve all these characteristics; they absolutely shine in their role.

Addressing each separate characteristic in turn, small is a given. Small is necessary. Small is what makes it hard to achieve all the other functions.

■ FLATNESS

Hideaway guns get exponentially easier to conceal with every fraction of an inch in width that they shed. The effect is enough to hurt your buddy's feelings when you demonstrate how much better your ultra-flat Sig P938 disappears than his Sig P250. Achieving a minimal width requires that semiautos be built around a single-stack magazine, which gives up high capacity. Unfortunately, a flat double-stack magazine just doesn't exist. But that's ok. It's a worthwhile tradeoff.

■ CONTROLLABLE

In semiautos, this vital characteristic (you'll have a very poor relationship with your constant companion if it hurts you every time you shoot it) is a matter of design and caliber choice. The best semiautos offer a "high" grip, bringing the center of the bore (which happens to be the point of maximum recoil thrust) as low as possible above your hand, minimizing its very powerful affect on muzzle rise.

Controllability and power—our next characteristic—are inseparably connected and weigh directly against each other. Caliber choice is pretty simple: bigger cartridges hit harder, but kick more—sometimes a lot more—and reduce magazine capacity. Once you've hit 9mm, bigger isn't always better. As long as you're willing to spend the dollars needed to stuff your carry magazines with premium defense ammo (more on this in Chapter 2), you're probably better off going with a 9mm that holds eight rounds and doesn't loosen your dental fillings every time you shoot it than with a .45 ACP that only holds six rounds and kicks like uncle George's mule. Caliber is a very personal choice though, and if you prefer to carry a .45, well, bless you. There are some darned good pistol options available in .45.

Controllability in revolvers is also affected by grip design, but to a lesser extent. Inherent weight and caliber influence shootability greatly, and there are some really difficult-to-shoot combinations out there. Smith & Wesson's compact snubnosed scandium-frame .357 Magnum, for example. Shooting it is about like turning a hand grenade wrapped in duct tape loose in your fist. Sure, it has a place, but it's not for everyone. If you want to carry a small revolver, balance weight with caliber carefully.

■ POWER

Power is perhaps the most hotly debated topic attached to concealed-carry handguns. Most experts agree that you should carry the most powerful personal protection handgun that you can control well and shoot accurately, whether it is a .380 or an evil-stomping magnum. For the most part, I agree, with some caveats. Popular, suitable semi-auto and revolver calibers and their strengths and weaknesses are discussed in detail in Chapter 2.

■ RELIABLE

This concept is very simple, yet can be very expensive. Simple because there's really no room for argument: any handgun for concealed carry absolutely must go bang every time the trigger is pulled. Shrugging off sweat, body humidity and oils, lint, dust, and a ton of underestimated mechanical challenges is a monumental demand.

Speaking of mechanical challenges, consider the physics: small, compact springs are required to function under-weight slides, and lock barrels into battery against leverage and angles focused by the diminutive space into which the whole mechanism is compressed. (By the by, revolvers suffer from none of this—which is one of the main reasons some knowledgeable people choose to carry them.) The whole must safely contain a controlled explosion every time the gun is fired. Entire magazine articles have been written on the reasons that compact semiautos are so hard to design for reliability. Suffice it to say here that some designs achieve that reliability; many do not. Several proven, popular models are reviewed in a later chapter.

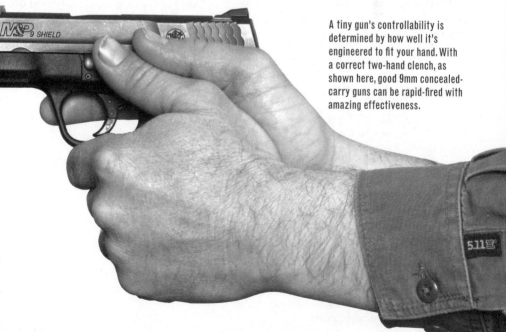

A tiny gun's controllability is determined by how well it's engineered to fit your hand. With a correct two-hand clench, as shown here, good 9mm concealed-carry guns can be rapid-fired with amazing effectiveness.

In a tiny handgun, power—as represented by the .45-caliber Springfield XDs at top—weighs against controllability, as represented in the 9mm-caliber Smith & Wesson M&P9 Shield at bottom. Some shooters prefer to hit hard, even at the expense of rapid follow-up shots.

Although this super-light scandium-frame revolver is chambered for .357 Magnum, shooters are usually better off carrying politer-recoiling .38 Special +P loads in it. In such a light gun full-house .357 Magnums recoil savagely, and there's no such thing as fast follow-up shots with them.

■ ACCURATE

Okay, okay. You've heard experts pontificate that accuracy isn't needed in a concealed-carry gun, because altercations usually take place at smell-the-villain's-breath distances. That's correct, to a point. And due to the mechanical challenges just discussed, designers frequently engineer in greater tolerances than would be optimum in a full-size pistol. That, coupled with the short sight radiuses and diminished grips of compact handguns, adds up to reduced accuracy. For the most part.

But it doesn't have to. Several of the particularly good choices available have proven to be very accurate. Two semiautos in particular, Smith & Wesson's M&P Shield and Kimber's Solo, will shoot groups smaller than a silver dollar at 10

Personal protection firearms have to offer absolute reliability. It's an engineering marvel that full-size handgun cartridges are shoehorned into tiny actions and still function without a hiccup.

Size affects accuracy less than a shooter's ability to shoot a gun with a mini handle and very short sight radius well. In the hands of a very capable shooter good concealed-carry guns will shoot groups like this at 10 yards.

yards. As for revolvers, I've got a J-Frame (compact) Smith & Wesson Model 60 with adjustable sights and a three-inch barrel with which I can hit a shoe box at 50 yards every shot.

If accuracy is available, shouldn't you have it? You never know when that belly gun may be called on to morph into a trail gun and help feed the family or knock off a predator.

Think that's far-fetched? My brother once used his Ruger SP101 compact .357 Magnum revolver to kill an aggressive, dominant Texas javelina that had been threatening his eight-year-old daughter. It was almost 50 yards away when he shot it.

Semiauto or revolver for concealed carry? The choice is yours... quality models of both are accurate and reliable.

AESTHETIC

Like anything we wear, we want our guns attractive. Sure, it's less important than any of the preceding characteristics, but let's face it, probably more concealed-carry guns are chosen for their looks than any other attribute. Such is human nature.

Aware of this foible, most manufacturers put a lot of effort into building beautiful handguns. So, by all means, choose a handgun that both can be counted on and makes you look good.

A selection of top-notch concealed-carry guns are reviewed and discussed in a later chapter.

NIGHTSTAND GUNS

Handguns that pull night duty are vastly varied. Most gun owners just use whatever they have or whatever they're most comfortable shooting. Those are both good reasons to use what you use, but the truth of the matter is, there are characteristics that make some handguns more suitable than others.

Those characteristics can be defined as the attributes that make for an honestly capable combat handgun. Attributes that will help you deal with whatever threats you may face when that bump in the night tells you that it's time to patrol the home front. Whether you end up facing a single assailant with deadly intent or a civilization-wide state of emergency caused by foreign invasion, you want that one handgun to be the most capable, versatile tool possible.

Face it. When given the choice of your compact, lightweight concealed-carry semiauto or snubnose revolver, or a 17-round full-size Glock 9mm or a 1911 .45 ACP, which would you want? You've got a drugged-up frothing-at-the-mouth murderer in your face, or an America without electricity, or a Katrina-level natural disaster warping the minds of your fellow man. I'll wager you'll pick up a powerful full-size handgun. Personally, if given time, I'll get dressed and stow my compact gun where it belongs, but the gun I grab from my nightstand will be big, bad, and really functional.

Full-size, high-capacity and/or powerful, controllable, reliable, accurate, and designed with a light rail (if a semiauto). It takes a good handgun to excel at all these demands, but such guns are much more common and available than their very specialized concealed-carry counterparts.

FULL SIZE

Full size is what allows a proper combat-capable handgun to be all it can be. Hand-filling grips aid recoil control and enhance rapid-fire capability. Generous magazine wells (the inside part of the grip that houses the magazine) provide room for high capacity magazines. Longer barrels offer accuracy-enhancing sight radius and aid velocity, which translates into more downrange energy and thus better projectile impact performance. And so on. Let's pick apart these desirables.

HIGH CAPACITY AND/OR POWERFUL

Many full-size guns hold from 12 to 19 rounds of ammunition—mostly in 9mm or .40 S&W caliber—and say what you will, capacity is your friend when the chips are down. I'm old-school, and would just as soon have an eight-round 1911 in .45 ACP because I believe in doing my darnedest to make every shot count, rather than going the spray-and-pray route. However, if you practice enough to build good shooting technique, and employ a little discipline, capacity is all good. Nobody can tell me that capacity is bad—whether you can't shoot worth beans and might have to spray a little to have a prayer, or you're a shooting protégé that can stop 17 individuals of murderous intent with your 17 cartridges, capacity is your friend.

In most cases, once a semiauto handgun reaches a certain capacity threshold, power and capacity don't mix (capacity is mostly a moot point in revolvers). There are some exceptions, but most guns in 9mm and .40 S&W will carry around 14 to 17 rounds, while most .45 ACPs will hold about eight cartridges. That's a tradeoff that has inspired many a barroom debate, and will continue to do so for a very long time.

America's most popular, long-lived semiauto pistol model is the John Browning-designed Model 1911. Originally built by Colt, it's now one of the most widely produced handguns in the world, and it deserves every bit of its popularity. In a nutshell, it's a single-action design (which makes a very clean, crisp trigger pull possible) employing a single-stack magazine that typically holds seven or eight rounds of .45 ACP (Automatic Colt Pistol) ammunition. The design features two safeties: one is a common-type thumb safety, the other is a grip safety (unless you are gripping the pistol, it cannot fire). When it comes to heavy-caliber semiauto pistols, most experts agree that the 1911 is one of the most shootable handguns in existence.

Popular high-capacity designs are almost a polar opposite to the 1911. Though metal-framed versions exist (Beretta's M9—currently in U.S. military service—and M92, and Sig

The tiny actions on concealed-carry guns provide a huge challenge to reliable function, particularly because of sharp barrel tilt when the slide is fully rearward, and because the slide has almost no acceleration distance before contacting the fresh cartridge in the magazine. In essence it has to push the cartridge into the chamber from a standing jump. Amazingly, quality concealed-carry guns are truly reliable—an underappreciated feat of engineering.

Sauer's fantastic P226 and P229 for example), most are built on polymer frames (Glocks and Smith & Wesson M&Ps, to name a couple of the best). I grew up with revolvers and 1911s, and it took me a very long time to come around to liking what some traditionalists call "Tupperware guns." But come around I did. I still love my 1911s more, but I must admit that I work my polymer-frame guns harder. They hold an incredible amount of ammunition, weigh a lot less than metal-framed handguns, and are as durable as a wheelbarrow. Most employ a striker-fired mechanism, which, though very robust, can never provide as clean, light, and crisp a trigger pull as a single-action design. In addition to high capacity, a big advantage of polymer-frame pistols is that most have a picatinny rail for mounting lights molded into the dust cover portion of the frame just in front of the trigger guard.

There are a few semiauto handguns that bridge the capacity/power gap. For the most part, they employ grips that are borderline to big for the average shooter's hand in order to squeeze double-stack .45 ACP magazines—and the resulting increase over single-stack mags—into the mag well. Almost all use polymer frames. Notable models are Springfield's XD45, Glock's G21SF, and Smith & Wesson's M&P45. All three hold 12 or 13 rounds of .45-caliber goodness in the magazine. If you've got big hands and love the .45 ACP caliber, get one, stick it in the drawer of your nightstand, and slumber like a baby, secure in the knowledge that you have both high capacity and mighty authoritative power standing the night watch.

■ CONTROLLABLE

Several things tame recoil, weight and grip design among the most important. Weight is the most effective, but a gun can get cumbersome if it's too heavy. You want a gun that is light enough to carry. I particularly like polymer-frame high capacity semiautos in the lighter calibers (9mm and .40 S&W), because they provide a good balance of an adequate cartridge that kicks comparatively little, plenty of rounds, and quite light weight. I'm also partial to a good metal-frame .45 ACP—the weight in the metal frame dampens recoil and aids quick follow-up shots—but they are heavier. An alloy-frame .45 ACP is a good compromise for a full-size gun that will be carried a lot.

> *Of course, to take advantage of a good high grip design, you've got to learn to hold the handgun with a good high grip.*

Grip design is a many-faceted thing, but most important to controlling recoil is how high it gets your grip in relation to the center of the bore. With any handgun, physics dictate that the closer the bore is to your hand, the more controllable muzzle jump will be. Sure, you can point out that the recoil energy has to go somewhere, and that if it's not leaping up as violently, the gun must be recoiling harder rearward. Point is: that's where you want it. Rearward recoil is, with a correct grip, very easy to control, even during rapid fire.

Designers today are pretty conscious of creating a model that handles recoil well, but there are still vast differences from model to model. Some of the best high grip designs are found on Smith & Wesson's M&P series, Glocks, and 1911s. Sig Sauers and Springfield XD and XDMs, though they are fine guns, lose points in comparison.

Of course, to take advantage of a good high grip design, you've got to learn to hold the handgun with a good high grip. I'm often taken aback by the number of folks I see that grab a handgun by the middle and end of the grip, rather than settling the grip nice and high.

Most current polymer models offer interchangeable grip panels, which can help position one's hand correctly, and enable the owner to fit the gun to his or her hand. Gimmicky? No. I always detested the way Glocks felt in my hand (though I had great respect for the gun itself), but my Gen 4 G17 with the smallest grip insert feels really good in my hand. Not just acceptable, but good. Grip inserts do make a difference.

■ RELIABLE

In full-size semiautomatic handguns of reasonably good design, it could accurately be said that almost all malfunctions are caused by one of two things: poor ammunition or faulty magazines. Assuming you use correct, high-quality ammunition, consistent malfunctions can usually be remedied simply by discarding the magazine or magazines causing the problem, and replacing them with top-quality mags.

(I'm not ignoring revolvers in this section, it's just that they don't suffer from bad magazines, and an owner has to try really hard to find ammo that won't function, or to physically screw up a revolver badly enough to make it malfunction-prone. Yet another reason to love revolvers!)

Other, less common causes are neglect, where the owner overlooks the need to clean and/or lubricate his or her firearm. A good, thorough cleaning and oiling works wonders on tired, abused semiautos. In a pinch, lacking the necessary tools for that thorough cleaning, just a good lavish oiling can get a pretty fouled up pistol back in action. Maintenance for high pistol and revolver performance is discussed in another chapter, along with down-and-dirty procedures for quickly getting a disastrously dirty gun running.

Why are full-size semiautos less prone to malfunctioning than the petite pistols we love to stuff into hiding on our person? Because engineering is not cramped by limited space. When the mechanics of a pistol don't have to be small enough to fit into a gun the size of a pack of cigarettes, design can focus on minor conveniences such as reliability-enhancing physics.

Case in point: slide travel is very effective when a slide retracts a good 3/8-inch or more behind the rear of the next heir-to-the-chamber in the magazine, and thus has plen-

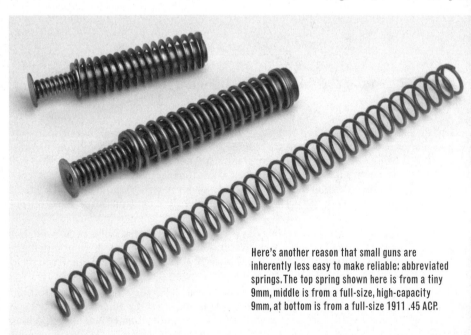

Here's another reason that small guns are inherently less easy to make reliable: abbreviated springs. The top spring shown here is from a tiny 9mm, middle is from a full-size, high-capacity 9mm, at bottom is from a full-size 1911 .45 ACP.

Full-size guns such as this Glock G17 would be far more suitable to survival in a decaying world than tiny concealed-carry guns. They carry more ammo and are easier to shoot accurate rapid-fire with.

tiful distance to accelerate prior to whanging into the rim of said cartridge and boosting it up the abrupt angle of the feed ramp. This is how most full-size semiautos are engineered.

Slide travel is not so effective when the limits of a tiny pistol only allow for 1/16-inch of rearward travel past the back of the next cartridge in the magazine—in which case it more or less just hooks the next cartridge in line and has to heave it up the feed ramp and into the chamber from a standing start. And of course, an itty-bitty coil spring, or often a coil spring inside a coil spring powers that short throw, because that's the only way to produce the needed energy within the space limitations. Very unlike the healthy zest of a full-size, full-power spring in a full-size handgun.

Less easy to understand is the degree of angle conundrum. A barrel must pivot, or tilt, in order to unlock from battery and to allow the empty casing from the previous round to be ejected. Now, not all semiautos use a tilting-barrel lockup, but many do. Consider that a barrel breech must drop a specified amount to fully clear the locking lug recesses, and must further tilt as the slide zips rearward to cough out the empty. In most cases, the fulcrum of that tilt is the point where the barrel emerges from the front of the slide: physics dictate that a shorter slide reduces the distance from the pivot point to the breach, and as a result the angle that the barrel must tilt is necessarily more acute. The shorter the barrel/slide, the greater the angle; the greater the angle, the lesser the inherent reliability.

When facing a potential deadly threat within the confines of your home, you're better off with a big gun that's easy to get the best out of than a small gun that you struggle to control.

The argument between power and capacity continues to rage, and always will. Most .45 ACPs hold 8-plus-1; high-capacity 9mms hold 17-plus-1. Both have valid advantages.

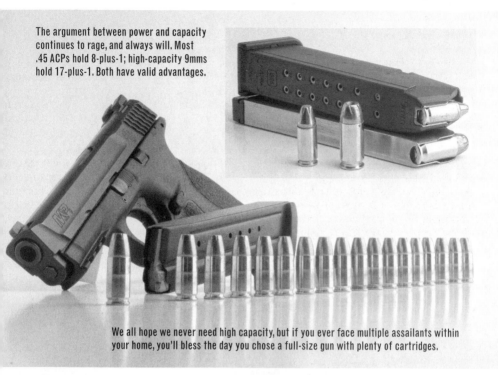

We all hope we never need high capacity, but if you ever face multiple assailants within your home, you'll bless the day you chose a full-size gun with plenty of cartridges.

John Browning's Model 1911 is the most popular pistol in America, and for good reason. That said, traditionally configured models (left) had a thumb safety and tang that could chew up your hand. Most modern 1911s have a protective beavertail grip safety and extended thumb safety that make them more shooter-friendly.

I love 1911s more, but I work my polymer-frame guns harder. They hold an incredible amount of ammunition, weigh a lot less than metal-framed handguns, and are as durable as a wheelbarrow.

A few polymer-frame guns bridge the gap between .45 ACP power and 9mm capacity. The Springfield XDm shown here contains 13-plus-1 rounds of hard-hitting .45 ammo.

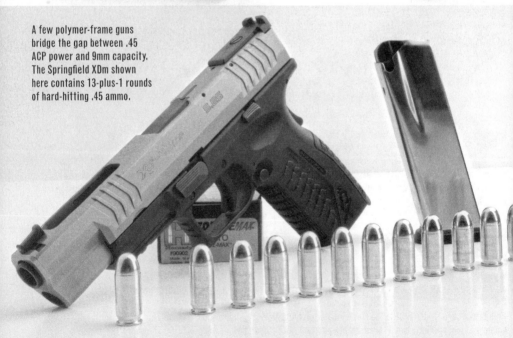

A high grip—meaning that you get the web between thumb and index finger crammed up hard against the top of the grip—enables you to control recoil. Beware the casual low-grip: the gun will come alive and try to leap out of your fist during recoil.

We all love the welterweights of the handgun world, and for good reason. They do a valiant job of defending us when crippled with reliability-destroying engineering parameters. We love 'em for it. But when the chips are down, if you've got the option of picking up a full-size handgun from your nightstand, by all means, do it. They are simply more reliable. End of argument.

ACCURATE

Contrary to popular opinion, short, compact handguns aren't necessarily less accurate than their full-size counterparts. Rather, they are simply harder for humans to shoot accurately. Locked in a machine, many compact guns shoot very accurately. Locked in a fist, full-size guns do much better.

Why? Two primary reasons. First, a full-size gun fills the hands better, making it easier to hold steady. Second, it has a longer sight radius (the distance between front and rear sights), making it much easier to achieve a consistent sight picture.

Grip inserts make a big difference in how a handgun fits your hand. While early-generation Glock pistols felt like a chunk of firewood in my hand, Gen 4 guns actually feel good.

Full-size guns are easy to make reliable. Note how far the slide travels rearward behind the cartridge; that distance provides acceleration before the slide picks up the fresh cartridge.

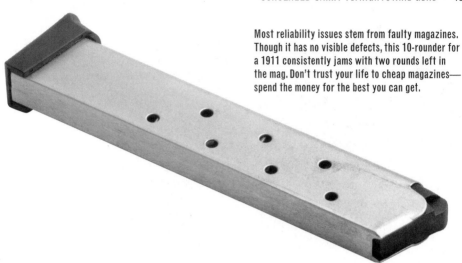

Most reliability issues stem from faulty magazines. Though it has no visible defects, this 10-rounder for a 1911 consistently jams with two rounds left in the mag. Don't trust your life to cheap magazines— spend the money for the best you can get.

There are influences of a smaller nature, such as the more freely pro- portioned trigger ergonomics that a full-size gun offers as opposed to the sometimes-cramped trigger feel of some compact guns, but they are negligible compared to hand-filling fit and sight radius.

How accurate should a good full-size handgun be? Traditional wisdom suggests that a defensive handgun should shoot groups measuring no more than four inches at 25 yards, when supported by a good sandbag rest. Fair enough, and most people may themselves struggle to shoot groups any tighter than that, but most of today's quality handguns will shoot groups half that size or even smaller in the hands of an expert precision handgunner. Premium custom guns will frequently shoot two-inch groups at 50 yards.

Although a good compact pistol can be very accurate, it's easier for a shooter to place accurate shots with a full-size gun— especially during the tremendous stress of a fight.

Sight radius plays a big part in how easy it is to milk accuracy out of a gun. Although with very careful shooting these two guns print similar groups, the bigger pistol with the longer sight radius is much easier to shoot well.

LIGHT RAILS

I used to mentally scoff at the concept of attaching a flashlight to the bottom of my handgun, but I kept my contempt to myself in case that attitude might eventually prove me an idiot. Good thing, too: I've grown into the realization that anyone who does not do all he can to have illumination—very, very powerful illumination—available during a potential nighttime encounter with a person of deadly intent is foolish indeed.

Louis L'Amour's books were a defining influence in my formative years, and one of the bits of gun lore that I've always retained is to always know what you're shooting at before you pull that trigger. I can think of nothing more horrible than shooting a family member or friend because a lack of visibility prevented me from identifying them.

Lights have advantages in addition to simple illumination. The one I like best is the way a correctly-handled tactical light utterly destroys the bad guys night vision while leaving the homeowner more or less unseen. A hundred lumens or more of LED light impacting one's darkness-dilated pupils tends to have a rather disorienting affect, and it takes several minutes for eyes thus disabled to regain vision.

Beautifully-built, high-end guns can be obscenely accurate, especially with ammunition they like. This is a five-shot group fired from a Nighthawk Custom 1911 Falcon. The elk-antler grips were a Christmas gift handmade by my brother. Without doubt, it's my favorite handgun.

Having light to identify and accurately shoot a deadly threat is important in the dark—don't blaze away at bumps in the night. Gun-mounted lights are the easiest and most controllable, but they do have down sides. You might "identify" your thirsty kid—with your gun aimed at him.

Be careful to avoid backsplashing light into your own eyes—and ruining your night vision. Don't accidentally shine a powerful tactical light against a nearby white wall.

I say correctly handled because the fellow holding the light can do the same to himself without care. This isn't a manual on tactical light manipulation; let it suffice to suggest avoiding backsplash (shining your light against a nearby white wall or other reflective surface) that could temporarily blind you.

Your light doesn't have to be attached to your handgun. Some folks don't like the feel of a light hanging off their pistol. Revolvers—unless something like a Smith & Wesson M&P R8, with a rail machined into or screwed onto the bottom of the barrel—are left in the dark when it comes to attaching handgun lights, tawdry pun intended. Good concealed-carry handguns are too small to support a light. Keeping a powerful hand-held tactical flashlight—activated with a pressure switch in the base—with your gun works well, as long as you take the time to learn how to hold the gun and light together and control the direction of the light's beam while firing in the dark.

> *Various types of firearm exist for good reason, and forethought and preparedness can fit you with the best tool for the job.*

That said, the simplest, most controllable way to combine a tactical light with your nightstand gun is without doubt to attach it to the rail on your handgun's dustcover (the

If your handgun
doesn't have a
light rail beneath
the barrel, or if
you simply prefer
using a hand-held
light, get a quality
high-lumen light
with a tail switch
and learn to hold it
properly and shoot
with it.

When searching a home for a threat, glance light off of a light-colored ceiling or wall to illuminate the whole room first, then search dark corners with the beam.

When I travel I generally take my Glock G17 with me, and I put a Surefire X300 light on it before placing it on the nightstand by my bed.

portion of the frame in front of the trigger guard), assuming your handgun has such a rail. This keeps the light always with your gun, and always pointing where your gun is pointing. Most appropriate lights have rocker or pressure-type switches that allow both constant-on and momentary-on use. Several quality lights, both hand-held and for rail mounting, are discussed in the chapter "Lights, Lasers, and Other Gizmos."

You may argue that having a light always point where the gun is pointing violates one of the laws of gun safety, and you might end up pointing your Glock at your sleepy teenager in an effort to identify him. That takes us back to the "correctly handled" concept: most effective use of a tactical light (for patrolling/searching your mansion) is by momentarily glancing the beam off of a ceiling or nearby wall in order to briefly illuminate a room. This technique both keeps the muzzle away from your astonished adolescent and provides best visibility.

It's worth noting that the ability to shine your light anywhere in the house while keeping your handgun pointed down or up—depending on whether your kids sleep upstairs or in the basement—is one of the few advantages offered by a non-gun-mounted light. Of course, then if you do suddenly need to shoot and desperately need the villain illuminated, you must be accomplished enough to bring the light and your gun's sights together. Quickly. Under extraordinary pressure.

IN SUMMARY: CONCEALED-CARRY VS. NIGHTSTAND GUNS

When it comes down to it, the ability to use whatever gun is available at the time of need is more important than exactly what type of gun it is. However, various types of firearm exist for good reason, and forethought and preparedness can fit you with the best tool for the job.

When choosing a handgun to conceal on your person, look for something that disappears easily, feels good in your hand, and is reliable and as powerful as you can comfortably shoot.

For a nightstand or home protection handgun, choose your tool for superb control, high capacity and/or power, reliability, durability, and accuracy. And stack a miniature spotlight on its undercarriage.

CHAPTER 4:

RECOMMENDED CONCEALED CARRY HANDGUNS

SEMIAUTOMATIC PISTOLS

SMITH & WESSON M&P SHIELD

When S&W engineers were tasked with designing a new concealed-carry polymer-frame pistol, they were given a seemingly impossible set of parameters. It had to be less than an inch wide, it had to be superbly controllable through recoil, it had to be comfortable in the hand, and it had to meet the incredibly demanding criteria of the M&P line.

You should trust and be comfortable with your concealed carry handgun. If ever called upon to use it in defense of life you don't want internal doubts about it.

Smith & Wesson M&P Shield

Unknown even to many serious gun folks, the M&P designation—for "Military & Police," isn't just a cute prefix; it indicates that the model has passed a set of reliability, accuracy, and endurance tests so rigorous that most handgun models are literally incapable of surviving them. As a result, models that earn the M&P designation are invariably robust, precise, and consistently accurate.

Smith & Wesson's engineers aren't among the best in the world for nothing. In the end, the M&P Shield—as the new compact pistol was named—both met the company's parameters and exceeded them in performance. I obtained one of the first 9mm versions to leave the factory, and in subsequent testing put over 1,000 rounds through it without a single hiccup and without cleaning or lubing it. I can shoot golf balls with it at 10 yards, and I can dump accurate rapid-fire strings shockingly fast for such a small gun. I've carried it concealed across thousands of miles of American soil. Incredibly, the S&W M&P Shield sells for $449 retail—if you can find one. As I write this, they are in such demand that the factory can't keep up, and buyers pay well over suggested retail for even a used one.

> *...incredibly well built, provides above-par performance, and costs less than a set of tires for the family sedan.*

Utilizing a hybrid single-stack magazine, the M&P Shield comes with two magazines: a short version for deep concealed carry, and a longer version that provides a full, three-finger grip and contains one more round than the short magazine. Capacity in 9mm is 7-plus-1 and 8-plus-1 rounds, respectively, and in .40 S&W it is 6-plus-1 and 7-plus-1 rounds, respectively. Shields have both a trigger "safety" and a low-profile thumb safety on the left side of the frame, and weigh 19 ounces, empty.

If asked to suggest the single best concealed-carry semiauto handgun available today, I'd have to say the Smith & Wesson M&P Shield. It's incredibly well built, provides above-par performance, and costs less than a set of tires for the family sedan. Kimber's Solo and

Sig Sauer's P938 rival it in performance and offer metal-frame elegance, but you'll pay almost double.

I've carried mine a number of ways, but currently my go-to rig is a Galco IWB holster.

Kimber Solo

■ KIMBER SOLO 9MM

Rivaled only by the Sig Sauer P938 for elegance, the Kimber Solo is an extraordinary combination of ergonomics and performance packed into a tiny, sleek, round-edged-and-cornered package. Though it is nominally of striker-fired design, the trigger mechanism is a hybrid and offers a pull more like that of a good single-action 1911 than any striker-fired trigger has any right to.

Function draws heavily on 1911 design as well. The Solo 9mm has an ambidextrous manual thumb safety in the classic 1911 position, and magazine release buttons as well.

The Solo achieves a petite 17 ounces (empty) by being the smallest 9mm semiauto that I'm aware of. Magazines hold six rounds, and Kimber suggests using premium 124- to 147-grain defense loads for most reliable function. Small size notwithstanding, all accounts I've heard reported outstanding accuracy.

This ain't your everyday workin' tool: prices range from $900 up to around $1,200. Don't let that fool you or deter you. The Kimber Solo is one of the best truly compact 9mm pistols available, and has panache enough to be at home in any Rolls Royce or Ferrari. While a Solo can be carried concealed any number of ways, it really deserves a fine inside-the-waistband holster of alligator or some other exotic leather.

■ SPRINGFIELD XDS .45 ACP

Probably the smallest really usable .45 semiauto available, the XDs shrinks down and incorporates the finest elements of its bigger siblings, the XD and XDm. The grip texture

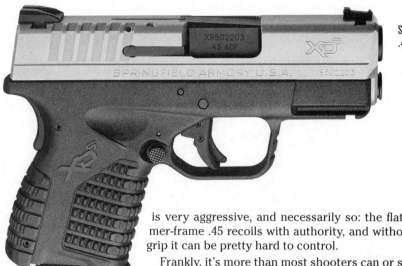

Springfield XDs
.45 ACP

is very aggressive, and necessarily so: the flat little poly-mer-frame .45 recoils with authority, and without a secure grip it can be pretty hard to control.

Frankly, it's more than most shooters can or should want to control. But for experienced handgunners with the train-ing and discipline to handle the recoil, and who want the power of the .45 cartridge in a tiny package, it's arguably the best option available. Like most polymer pistols, it has a safety incorporated into the trigger. More importantly—and a feature I really like—it has a 1911-type grip safety. In essence, until you grasp the gun and your palm depresses the grip safety, it cannot fire.

Capacity is five rounds in the magazine, plus one in the chamber for a total of six rounds. Weight is just under 22 ounces, empty, and suggested retail price is $599, though street price is somewhat lower.

■ P938 & P238

Styled like a scaled-down 1911, the 9mm P938 and .380 ACP P238 from Sig Sauer are mar-vels of sophisticated engineering for ergo-nomics, aesthetics, and performance. If you are a dedicated 1911 guy or gal, strongly consider one of these two models as your concealed-carry sidearm. The controls—slide stop, mag release, and ambidextrous safe-ty—are all located in 1911-esque fashion, and the single-action design makes for a fantastic, crisp, creep-free trigger. There is, by the way, no 1911-type grip safety.

SIG P938
& P238

Weighing only 16 ounces (P938), and 15 ounces (P238), with capacities of 6-plus-1, these are proper pocket pistols, but feel great in the hand, point well, and are both accurate and reliable. Add excellent workmanship and class enough for Frank Sinatra, and you get the picture. The P938, in particular, ranks in my top two or three concealed-carry models. They are, however, expensive, ranging around $800 suggested retail.

Beretta Nano

BERETTA NANO

Though it appears a bit blocky at first, the Nano is well contoured and sleek in function. Incredibly flat at 0.90 inch, it carries comfortably and operates reliably. The magazine release is reversible for southpaw shooters, and the sights are easily adjusted with a hex wrench. Simple disassembly makes for easy maintenance—even the laziest shooters among us have no excuse for leaving their Nano dirty.

Carrying 6-plus-1 rounds of 9mm ammunition and weighing only 18 ounces, it is a bit of a handful in recoil, but manageable. Like most of its ilk, it has a trigger-shoe-type safety, but no manual thumb safety. At a suggested retail price of $475, it's one of the better options available for folks needing solid performance for a good value.

GLOCK G26

I am not currently and have never been a fan of short, fat pistols (using double-stack magazines) for concealed carry. Merely lopping off an inch of barrel and a finger's-worth of grip doesn't make a gun concealable. In my college days behind the counter of the local gun shop, I saw more compact and sub-compact double-stack polymer handguns come back for trade-in six weeks after they were purchased than any other type of gun.

Glock G26

What did the disenchanted owner trade for? A full-size model of the same pistol, or a flat, single-stack, truly concealable semiauto of some description.

All that said, the 9mm G26 is a pretty good pistol, if you can find someplace about your person in which to make it disappear. The double-stack magazine holds 10-plus-1 rounds, and unloaded the G26 weighs only 20 ounces, which isn't much more than similar single-stack guns such as the S&W M&P Shield, Sig Sauer P938, and Beretta Nano. Predictably, the only safety is Glock's Safe Action trigger. If you opt for the Gen 4 version, you'll get a reversible, enlarged magazine catch and modular, interchangeable back straps.

How wide is it? 1.18 inches. Almost a full third-inch more than, for instance, the Beretta Nano, and a couple of tenths wider than the S&W M&P Shield, Springfield XDs, and others. Prices run in the high $500s.

KIMBER 1911 SUPER CARRY PRO

Legendary, historic, and capably carrying the honor of being the most successful semiautomatic pistol design ever, the 1911 inspires cult-like loyalty among a tremendous number of handgunners. Today, dozens upon dozens of different manufacturers produce 1911s of varying quality and characteristics. This is one of only two or three pistols that actually makes the transition from decent concealed-carry sidearm to fully adequate nightstand gun.

Though I've carried full-size, steel-framed 1911s concealed for months on end, I would no longer do so if I had the option of carrying a "commander-size" model, with a round or bobbed butt, built on an alloy frame. The commander-length barrel (four inches) conceals well but is long enough to function with 100-percent reliability, and offers decent velocity and enough sight radius for accurate shooting. As for the round, or bobbed, butt, I think it was Ed Brown that originally started the trend, and it makes enough of a difference that other manufacturers began designing similar—but different enough to avoid infringement complications—frames.

Note that I've described a configuration type. Any 1911 of quality manufacturer that fits the parameters outlined will carry and serve well. If you can afford to spring the dollars required to purchase the Ed Brown model that started the round-butt trend, by all means do so! You'll never regret it.

Kimber 1911
Super Carry Pro

I've listed the Kimber Super Carry Pro here because it's a well-made, beautifully finished example of the type, and one that is both a good value for the cost and with which I have extensive personal experience. Weight is right at 28 ounces, empty; it comes with tritium night sights with a machined "cocking shoulder" that allows you to function the slide one-handed by hooking the rear sight over your belt, a steering wheel, or whatnot; and the trigger pull will be good to exceptional right out of the box. Suggested retail price is $1,596, but real-world price is lower. As a rule, quality 1911s are expensive, but this one is worth every penny and offers a lot of very nice features for the price.

REVOLVERS

■ SMITH & WESSON J-FRAMES

The "J" frame is the smallest of the Smith & Wesson revolver frames. Almost any .38 Special or .357 Magnum handgun built on it makes for an excellent concealed carry sidearm, with the exception of the odd model with a four- or five-inch barrel. All models in the calibers above have five-shot cylinders, so they don't exactly offer endless firepower.

I've carried a .357 Magnum Model 60 J-frame with a three-inch barrel and adjustable sights on many a backcountry foray, and it's one of my favorite J-frame options. It offers excellent accuracy and authority in a pistol that shrugs off the most brutal abuse Mother Nature can throw at it, and it's about the only J-frame I've shot that is actually fairly comfortable in recoil with .357 Magnum loads, courtesy of the longer barrel and decently-heavy steel frame.

My other favorites are the snub-nosed, alloy-framed Model 637 and Model 340. The first is chambered in .38 Special, and costs around $460—a very good value for such a capable, high-quality concealed-carry revolver. The second is chambered in .357 Magnum, and of course will fire .38 Specials as well. More advanced alloys are required in order to handle the greater pressures generated by the magnum cartridge, resulting in a much higher price: $800. It's worth it for guys who want the option of the greater terminal performance of the magnum cartridge, but I don't recommend it for any but the most experienced, recoil-insensitive shooters. Though it recoils quite pleasantly with .38s, the

Smith & Wesson J-Frame

darn thing feels like a grenade gone bad in your hand when you turn it loose with .357 Magnums.

If you wish to carry a revolver, these are my go-to suggestions. Most Smith & Wesson revolvers have quite smooth actions, excellent trigger pulls, and function perfectly and reliably. There are other options that are perhaps as good, but none better.

■ RUGER SP101

Rugers are known for being overbuilt, tougher than the rest, and capable of digesting a diet of full-bore magnum loads without experiencing significant wear. Additionally, they are built on cast frames of generous dimension, making them slightly heavier than competing models. This is both negative and positive—they're less comfortable to carry, but the added mass dampens recoil. If you're determined to shoot .357 Magnums in a compact revolver, this is your pocket poison.

Like S&W J-frames, .357 Magnum models hold five rounds in the cylinder. My preference is the version with a three-inch barrel. Why? Because in reality they are about as easy to conceal as one with a two-inch barrel, and they offer better velocity and are easier to shoot well by virtue of the longer sight radius.

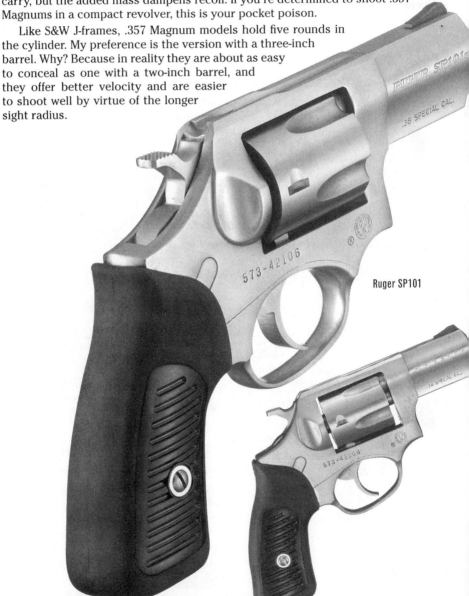

Ruger SP101

Some owners like to have an action job done to lighten the trigger, but I've always found that SP101s have quite satisfactory triggers. Putting several hundred rounds through one tends to slick up any roughness, if indeed present.

Not that other compact revolvers are wimpy when the going gets tough, but this is probably the toughest of them all. For continuous use in brutal environments, the SP101 is a premium option.

COLT DETECTIVE SPECIAL

If vintage class lifts your bubble and you want a compact revolver to carry, consider a Colt Detective Special. This is the gun that put snub-nosed pocket revolvers—as a type—on the map.

Colts utilize a flat, traditional mainspring. Known for incredibly smooth actions, they aren't perhaps quite as reliable and durable as the coil springs utilized by competing models.

If you wear genuine Harris Tweed jackets, or shun any shirts but those with French Cuffs, the only way you'll be entirely satisfied with your concealed carry revolver is by searching out and purchasing a used Detective Special in pristine condition.

Colt Detective
Special

CHAPTER 5:

RECOMMENDED NIGHTSTAND GUNS

SEMIAUTOMATIC PISTOLS

GLOCK G19 AND G17

Many are the handgun models that have stood night guard beside my bed, but the one currently drafted into service is a Gen 4 Glock G17.

Why that one? Because it's easy for me to shoot rapidly and accurately, because it holds 17 rounds in its magazine, and because my Surefire X300 light fits it beautifully. Among other reasons.

Glock G17: Most full-size handguns make good nightstand guns. It's hard to go wrong with any hand-filling, reliable pistol that accepts a weapon light.

For many years I thought Glocks were ugly, and that they had a much-too-drastic grip angle that caused me to point high, and that the square-ish grips felt like holding a piece of 2x4 lumber. (I still think that about the 1st, 2nd, and 3rd generation versions, but I really like the feel of the 4th generations.) I didn't like the fact that they had polymer frames, either. I'd been brought up on blued steel and big cartridges, and wondernines held no appeal to me.

I learned to respect Glocks through forced use. In my business, one gets thrown into contact with about every type of firearm available, and one must attempt objectivity. Once it dawned on me that I'd never seen a Glock jam (still haven't, though I know it happens on rare occasion), and that with a correct grip they could be ferociously fast and accurate, I came around. Like followed respect, and now my Glock 17 is one of the two most-used handguns in my possession. (The other is my Nighthawk Custom Falcon 1911.)

Gaston Glock was an idiosyncratic man with some shocking perversions in his character, but he engineered a handgun of pure genius. Simple, robust, accurate, light, and reliable, it ushered in a new age of semi-automatic handguns, and still is—in my opinion—one of the two best polymer-frame high-capacity pistols available. (The other is the Smith & Wesson M&P9.)

Here's a look at my three favorite holsters for carrying full-size guns: At left is a Galco Royal Guard—the best inside-the-waistband (IWB) holster I've used for big pistols; at center is a Blackhawk! Serpa CQC—a comfortable, good-looking retention holster; and at right is a Galco Concealable Belt Holster—in this case an alligator-hide version from the company's exotic line. If forced to choose just one, I'd take the Concealable Belt Holster.

There is no safety on a Glock, at least not in the usual sense. However, the trigger is dubbed a "safe action" trigger, and is meant to prevent accidental discharge. The trigger has a small compressible lever contained within the main trigger shoe, and unless it is compressed the trigger cannot travel rearward. This reduces the likelihood of catching the edge of the trigger on the lip of a holster or whatnot and firing the gun accidentally. Theoretically, unless the shooter's trigger finger is on the trigger, it won't go off. Sound in principle, but it does demand responsibility and safe gun handling practices by the shooter. Keep that finger away from the trigger unless you're ready to shoot.

Glocks do have some foibles. One, for instance, is the fact that the "unsupported" chamber (meaning that the rearmost portion of the chamber does not fully enclose the base of the cartridge) allows considerable case expansion upon firing, and those considerably expanded cases can be tricky to reload. Another is the rifling, which is polygonal in nature, and does not play nice with most cast lead bullets. You're much better off sticking with jacketed or copper plated bullets in your Glock.

My preference is the 9mm G17, with a 17-round capacity, closely followed by the G19, with a 15-round capacity and a slightly shorter frame. I don't get warm fuzzies over the .40 S&W cartridge—personally I consider it less than a .45 in power and less than a 9mm in capacity, thus a hybrid that attempts to fill the function of both yet fails to match either. However, it is a good cartridge, and for admirers of the .40 S&W, the G22 is really hard to beat.

I don't recommend messing around much modifying a Glock. The reason they have such a stellar reputation for reliability is that the factory design and parts work, and work every time. The only two mods that I occasionally suggest are to fit a Ghost aftermarket trigger with a lighter pull and an overtravel stop, and to replace the plastic factory sights with metal ones, preferably night sights with tritium inserts.

Finally, Glocks are a very good value when you go to exchange your hard-earned dollars for a personal protection tool. Standard models, new, bring around $550 to $580; guns in good used condition can be had for around $400.

I carry mine two ways: for common belt carry I use a Blackhawk! Serpa CQC; and when I really want to carry a high-capacity full-size gun as my hideaway, I'll stow it inside my waistband in a Galco Royal Guard. I can only go six or eight hours with it there before my back and hip start complaining, but that's usually enough time to get me through whatever I was doing.

■ SMITH & WESSON M&P

The full-size M&P (Military & Police) semiauto is arguably the most ergonomic polymer-framed pistol ever designed.

That's a pretty lofty statement, but it's well founded. M&Ps are extraordinarily comfortable in the hand, and they come with three different-size grip inserts to finesse the grip size until it is just perfect for the owner's hand. The grip angle is the result of intensive research on the natural angle of the human fist in relation to the arm, resulting in a pistol that points itself as naturally as granny's naughty-finger when you're caught with your hand in the cookie jar. The grip itself is very high in relation to the axis of the bore, minimizing muzzle jump and enabling the shooter to control recoil well.

Once, at a bowling pin match, I borrowed a Pro-Series M&P9 from a buddy. Three times the buzzer went, and three times I cleared a rack of five pins in astonishing (even to myself) time, for the lowest aggregate of the day. I won the match with that pistol, even though I'd never shot it before. That says something about the ergonomics of the design. And no, at the time I didn't own and never had owned an M&P. Needless to say, it didn't take me long to purchase one after that.

In addition to being engineered for absolute reliability under the most adverse conditions imaginable, Smith & Wesson's M&P semiautos have two unusual features. First,

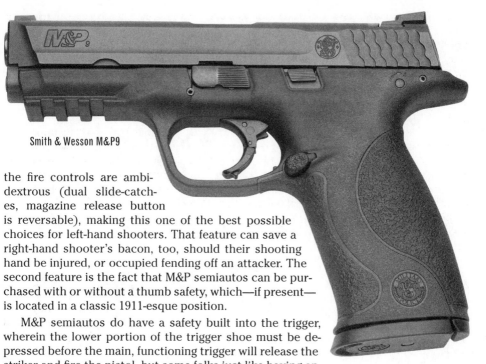

Smith & Wesson M&P9

the fire controls are ambidextrous (dual slide-catch-
es, magazine release button
is reversable), making this one of the best possible
choices for left-hand shooters. That feature can save a
right-hand shooter's bacon, too, should their shooting
hand be injured, or occupied fending off an attacker. The
second feature is the fact that M&P semiautos can be purchased with or without a thumb safety, which—if present—
is located in a classic 1911-esque position.

M&P semiautos do have a safety built into the trigger,
wherein the lower portion of the trigger shoe must be de-
pressed before the main, functioning trigger will release the
striker and fire the pistol, but some folks just like having an
external, positive, separate safety that will prevent a gun from going off even if the trigger finger is inadvertently placed on the trigger. Highly experienced defensive shooters
religiously practice indexing the trigger finger against the side of the frame until fully
intending to shoot, but most gun owners aren't highly experienced defensive shooters.
Personally, I rather like the external thumb safety. Having cut my teeth on a 1911, I'm accustomed to a thumb safety, and if one is present I instinctively activate it and deactivate
it as needed. The choice is yours: if you feel safer with an external safety, by all means
purchase your M&P with one. If you think you may someday forget to disengage it when
time wasted equals death, purchase your M&P without one.

Like most polymer-framed pistols, it is of striker-fired design and, though usable, triggers tend to be spongy and not particularly light. Having an Apex aftermarket trigger—
available through Brownells and other parts suppliers—installed helps, but recognize
that no M&P will ever equal a good single-action trigger.

Many versions exist in 9mm, .40 S&W, and .45 ACP, offering various sights, barrel
lengths, colors, and so on, and all of them have a light rail on the dust cover in front of
the trigger guard. Speaking specifically of the full-size models, you can't go wrong with
any of the variations. Prices are comparable to Glocks; new M&Ps can be had for $560
to $700, depending on bells and whistles, and good used versions can be purchased for
around $400.

Though my M&P9 "L" (long slide version) usually resides in my 72-hour emergency kit
or bums around to various 3-gun shoots with me, when I carry it I typically use a Galco
Concealable Belt Holster.

SPRINGFIELD XDm

A refinement of the very popular XD pistol, the "M" version is sleeker and perhaps a
bit lighter, depending on variation. I like how it looks better, too. Made in Croatia, these
semiautos have gained a huge following courtesy of good prices and solid performance.

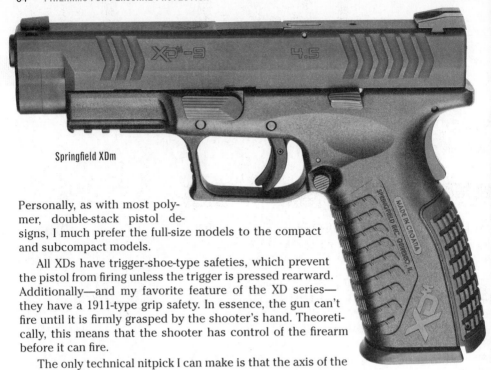

Springfield XDm

Personally, as with most polymer, double-stack pistol designs, I much prefer the full-size models to the compact and subcompact models.

All XDs have trigger-shoe-type safeties, which prevent the pistol from firing unless the trigger is pressed rearward. Additionally—and my favorite feature of the XD series— they have a 1911-type grip safety. In essence, the gun can't fire until it is firmly grasped by the shooter's hand. Theoretically, this means that the shooter has control of the firearm before it can fire.

The only technical nitpick I can make is that the axis of the bore is—as polymer pistols go—somewhat high above the grip, making for a design with more muzzle jump than others.

While I like the 9mm (with it's outstanding 19-plus-1 capacity) and .40 S&W versions, I particularly like the .45 ACP version with it's 13-plus-1 capacity. It's one of the better-feeling high-capacity .45s I've fired. Price runs around $550, depending on accessories.

Ruger SR9

RUGER SR9 & SR40

Retailing at $529, with a street price of under $500, the Ruger SR9 is probably the least-expensive polymer-frame pistol that—in my opinion—really makes the "depend your life on it" grade.

Technically, it's a striker-fired pistol engineered for reliability and good recoil control. The axis of the bore is low against the hand, helping maximize muzzle control during rapid fire.

Containing 17-plus-1 cartridges, it offers ergonomic concessions such as a reversible backstrap and ambidextrous safety and magazine release. Endurance tests by abusive gunwriters have proved it robust and capable. While it's available in .40 S&W and .45 ACP, my preference is 9mm.

SIG P226

SIG P220

SIG SAUER P226 & P229

This handgun takes us from the realm of polymer frame pistols to that of metal frames. In my opinion, no polymer-framed handgun ever has or ever will balance as well as a good metal-framed model, and Sig's P226 is one of the most ergonomic of them all. It's sibling model, the P229, has a slightly shorter barrel, but is an excellent pistol too.

Of double/single action design, these Sig pistols employ a decocker for safe carry. Translation: When a cartridge is chambered by working the slide, the external hammer is left cocked; pulling down on a lever on the left of the slide, about where a typical manual thumb safety would be located, drops the hammer without firing the cartridge. If the pistol should be needed in a hurry, a long, heavy double-action (both cocks and then fires—thus "double" action) trigger pull will cock the hammer and fire the pistol. Every shot thereafter will be single-action, since the slide leaves the hammer cocked after kicking out the spend cartridge case and chambering a fresh round. If the shooter ceases shooting before the magazine is empty, pulling on the decocker will lower the hammer to the safe position again.

I can't stress enough what a quality pistol Sig builds, as long as you stay with the metal-framed versions. I'm not partial to the company's polymer-frame guns: not that they're bad, it's just that the metal-frame guns are so good.

Capacity is 15-plus-1 rounds for the P226, 13-plus-1 for the P229, and price starts just under $1,000. That said, street price is usually considerably lower. Optional night sights are available, and highly recommended.

SIG SAUER P220

Imagine a big brother to the Sig P226 with a single-stack magazine in .45 ACP, and you've got the P220. Of very ergonomic, shootable design, and carrying 8-plus-1 cartridges, the P220 is in my opinion second only to the classic 1911 in .45-caliber pistol design; indeed it offers a couple of features that many shooters prefer, such as the decocker, easier disassembly, and so on.

It's a full-size fighting pistol. In other words, unless you've the stature of an NFL player, don't bother attempting to stash it away out of sight on your person. Price starts around $993, and runs up from there depending on options.

Remington 1911 R1

◼ MODEL 1911 (VARIOUS MAKES)

Without a doubt the most popular, legendary semiauto of all time, the 1911 is also the longest-lived. It entered life with U.S. armed services shortly before WWI, fought through WWII, Korea, Viet Nam, and other conflicts until the Beretta M9 replaced it for Army use in 1984. The 1911 continues to soldier on as the official sidearm of the U.S Navy, making it the handgun with the longest continuous service life in history.

Why is it so well loved? In short, it's incredibly ergonomic, is easy to manipulate while under stress, and is very robust and reliable. 1911 handguns made in recent decades tend to be very accurate, too. John Browning designed the 1911, and there's no arguing the fact that he was the most talented, influential firearm designer of all time.

The 1911: ergonomic, easy to manipulate while under stress, robust, and reliable.

Ithaca 1911

Cabot 1911

Many sizes of the 1911 exist, from little three-inch-barreled compact models up to six-inch long-slide versions, in calibers from .22 Long Rifle to .45 ACP and even bigger. For personal protection purposes, my recommendation is to stick with a full-size, steel-frame model in .45 ACP. It's what Browning designed, and it's the most balanced of the lot in mechanical function.

Alloy-frame models are popular among folks intending to carry a 1911 concealed, and make a good option, as do "Commander" versions, with a four-inch barrel. My favorite 1911 carry gun is just that, an alloy-

Kimber Desert Warior 1911

framed Commander with a rounded butt, in .45 ACP. However, for a proper nightstand or full-on disaster-handling gun, the full-size, steel-framed versions tame recoil better and offer the utmost in reliability.

Most experts agree that not only is the .45 ACP the most reliable cartridge in the 1911, it makes the most sense. If you're set on shooting a 9mm or .40 S&W, get something with a double-stack magazine. (There are adaptations of the 1911 that accept double-stack magazines—some of them very good—but at its best the 1911 is a single-stack design.)

One perceived drawback for a dedicated nightstand gun is the lack of a light-mounting rail on most 1911s. If it concerns you, get one with a rail—they are available from most major manufacturers. Otherwise, just learn to pair it with a good hand-held tactical flashlight, which is what I do.

When carrying, I either use a Royal Guard IWB holster or a Concealable Belt Holster by Galco Leather.

REVOLVERS

Not a lot of revolvers make what I consider great nightstand or full-blown, apocalyptic-scenario sidearms. Those that do are double-actions in .357 Magnum caliber, with four- to six-inch barrels. Much as I love the bigger .44 and .41 magnums, they are just too hard for the average shooter to shoot well and shoot quickly. Good medium-size, steel-frame revolvers in .357 Magnum are powerful, easy enough to shoot even with full-house loads, accurate, and reliable. Here are a few of the best.

■ RUGER GP100

Overbuilt for pure durability, the GP100 will take as many full-pressure magnum loads as you care to feed it without issue. One of the heavier mid-size double-action revolvers, it's easy to shoot because that weight tames recoil. Triggers can be heavy and sometimes a bit rough—if you purchase one and the trigger doesn't smooth up within 500 rounds or so, you may want to consider having a professional trigger job done.

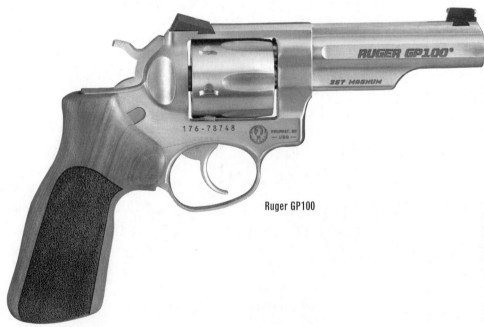

Ruger GP100

Capacity is six rounds, and weight is a hefty 40 ounces. Like most revolvers, GP100s don't have a light rail, so pair it with a good tactical flashlight. Though suggested retail for the blued model is nearly $700, and the stainless model tops $750, street price is usually much lower. It's a lot of gun for the money.

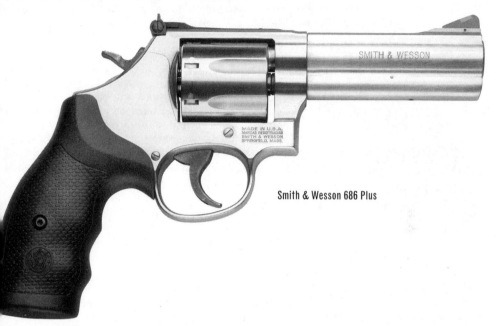

Smith & Wesson 686 Plus

■ SMITH & WESSON MODEL 586 PLUS

There are those who would disagree, but I consider the S&W 686 Plus to be arguably the single most versatile, ergonomic .357 Magnum revolver available. The dead-reliable actions are smooth, trigger pull is crisp and clean, and they are typically very accurate. Add to that the "plus" feature—an additional round in the cylinder, making it a seven-shooter—and you've got a fantastic all-around double-action revolver.

All 686 models are constructed of stainless steel, and are robust and durable enough to pound nails with and then go outshoot your buddies at the local bowling pin revolver match. Weight of the four-inch model is just over 38 ounces. Paired with a good tactical flashlight, it will serve yeoman's duty on your nightstand. They aren't cheap: suggested retail price is $849. The only double-action revolver that could possibly be better is its suped-up, combat-configured sibling, the S&W M&P R8.

■ SMITH & WESSON MODEL M&P R8

This is a state-of-the-art fighting revolver, and much as I love the slightly smaller L-framed model 686, the N-frame, eight-shot double-action M&P R8 is a better personal-protection gun. The "R8" designation indicates to characteristics vital to its superiority: a light rail machined into the barrel shroud, and eight-round capacity.

Designed from the ground up for duty carry and combat, the eight-shot cylinder is cut for moon clips (which allow shooters to reload very quickly), but functions just fine with loose rounds too, courtesy of the rimmed design of the .357 cartridge. Built on a scandium alloy frame with a stainless cylinder, the M&P R8 is light—only 36 ounces— and is completely finished in matte-black.

Smith & Wesson M&P R8

I once ran a series of rather challenging tests on an M&P R8, and it performed impressively in every department. One of the most memorable was the series of 100-yard groups I fired with a handgun scope mounted; they measured between 3.5 and 5.0 inches with a variety of ammo—very good accuracy indeed.

Pushing the high $1,200s, it's not cheap, but it will be accurate, smooth, and tough. Get a handful of moon clips for it, learn to use them, pair it with a good light such as SureFire's X400, and you'll have one of the most unstoppable nightstand and SHTF guns anywhere.

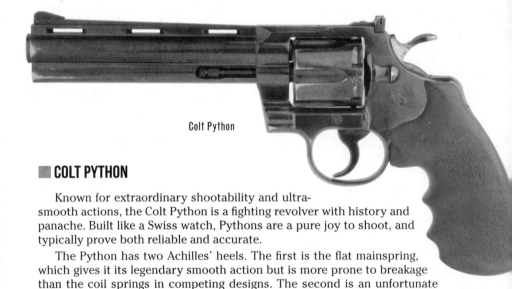

Colt Python

▮ COLT PYTHON

Known for extraordinary shootability and ultra-smooth actions, the Colt Python is a fighting revolver with history and panache. Built like a Swiss watch, Pythons are a pure joy to shoot, and typically prove both reliable and accurate.

The Python has two Achilles' heels. The first is the flat mainspring, which gives it its legendary smooth action but is more prone to breakage than the coil springs in competing designs. The second is an unfortunate byproduct of time: Pythons haven't been made for many years; most are coveted and protected to the point where they are not shot much any more, and as a result, gunsmiths adept at tuning, timing, and repairing them are becoming few in number.

If you drive a classic convertible, carry a pocket watch, and smoke a pipe, your only real choice (aside from a vintage Colt 1911 semiauto) is a Colt Python. They cost, but they bring refinement and charisma to the defensive revolver world.

CHAPTER 6:

CHOOSING THE RIGHT HANDGUN

C hoosing the one perfect handgun is like picking the perfect pair of shoes. While some models are very versatile indeed, nothing can fill every purpose.

As you may have gathered while perusing the previous chapters, I'm of the opinion that every gun owner interested in personal protection should possess two handguns (minimum): one slim, compact pistol for concealed carry, and one full-size pistol for use in every scenario other than those that dictate discretion in your possession of a sidearm. In other words, a handgun capable of handling serious, multiple-threat scenarios; end of days stuff—you know, severe natural disasters, the breakdown of civilization, the apocalypse.

Though I've said that a compact, concealable handgun is more suitable for pulling nightstand duty than a full-size handgun is of being properly concealed, if you must choose just one handgun, go with a truly combat-capable full-size model.

Why? For several reasons. For one thing, if you're a beginner, or even if you're very familiar with long guns—rifles and shotguns—but less so with handguns, a full-size hand-

No single handgun can or should fill every possible purpose, but with the myriad models available, anybody can find one just right for their needs.

Different physiques and levels of strength can dictate what works best for you. If you struggle to function the slide of a semiauto, you'll really struggle during the duress of a violent attack. Consider a revolver.

gun is much more easily mastered than a compact gun. It fills the hand better, holds steadier, and recoils less. For another, a full-size gun offers considerably more capacity—ammunition wise—and/or power. And it's usually easier to mount a light on. The list goes on.

> *When sallying forth to choose a gun, remember this: all those available models exist for good reason.*

However, I'm really going to lobby towards owning that two-gun minimum. Picking those two guns from the plethora of available, suitable models can be mind-boggling and, quite frankly, discouraging. There are so many models and manufacturers, and so many friends and salesmen with fervent, radically-differing opinions, that picking the best one can become daunting.

When sallying forth to chose a gun, remember this: all those available models exist for good reason—people have different likes and needs. Those preferences and needs are dictated by differing physiques, sizes, strengths, ages, and shooting experience, not to mention expected demands on the gun itself. So keep an open, objective mind; avoid very cheap guns (you really do get what you pay for in the gun world); and make your final decision based on what you personally like best. As long as it is a proven model with a reputation for reliability, made by a well-known, stand-by-their-product kind of manufacturer, pick what feels comfortable in your hand, points well, and is intuitive for you to operate.

Ideally, of course, you'll shoot a variety of models before settling on one. If possible, go out with friends, or go to a range that rents handguns, and try them out. Doing so will help you settle on the right gun pretty quickly. However, for many folks, that's just not an option. No sweat, take your time in the local gun shop, handle as many models as catch your eye, ask lots of questions, and narrow it down to the one you like the best and inherently trust the most. You'll make a good decision.

Here are a few considerations based on different physical human characteristics, experience levels, and expected needs.

HUMAN PHYSIQUE AND HANDGUN FIT

During my days behind a gun counter while working my way through college, a celebrity with acute physical handicaps came in. Clearly interested in AR-15s, partly because the shortest position of a collapsible stock on an M4 type rifle made it physically possible for him to shoulder a rifle, he unfortunately lacked the hand strength to either function the charging handle or hold the rifle in the firing position. Worse, every semiauto handgun he handled was too stiff—he didn't have the grip to draw the slide back. Disgruntled, he left the shop, refusing to consider the only sidearm that would likely have worked for him—a revolver.

Now, that's an extreme case, but I learned a great deal about the importance of both gun fit and attitude that day. You've got to find a gun that is right for you—one that you can manipulate with ease, hold steadily, and shoot comfortably—and once you've found that gun, you've got to mentally accept it and become proficient with it even if it is not what you'd originally wanted. Heck, I'd like to be able to sprint up and down mountains toting a 31-pound .50-caliber Barrett M82, but it's not going to happen. I do just fine with my M1A or my AR-15.

Let's consider a few rather useful clichés:

▓ WOMEN TEND TO BE SMALLER AND HAVE LESS HAND STRENGTH THAN THE AVERAGE MAN.

Deduction: Heavy handguns and semiautos with powerful mainsprings are not suitable. I don't care if you can wrestle the slide back on a big .45, ladies, you can't depend on it unless you can flick it back with sweaty, trembling hands in the most adrenaline-charged situation you can imagine. No matter your gender, find a handgun that feels good and points well for you, and that you can operate comfortably in dicey situations.

▓ AGE CAN PLAY A BIG PART IN HANDGUN CHOICE.

My much-loved stepfather was a jockey in his younger days, and as tough an hombre as you'll ever see. As Louis L'Amour, the favorite author of my youth, would have said, "He'd charge hell with a bucket of water." He recently traded me his .40-caliber Ruger SR9 for a .38 revolver. The honorable patina of years—and a couple of busted-up shoulders—removed from him the ability to withdraw the slide on his semiauto pistol. He was smart enough to roll with the times and get something that is comfortable for him to shoot. Even though he's in his mid-eighties now, I'm pretty sure that he and that .38 will handle any potential trouble at he and mom's home.

▓ GRIP SIZE AFFECTS HOW WELL YOU SHOOT A PARTICULAR HANDGUN.

In reality, it absolutely does. Unless you're so accomplished that you can literally pick up any handgun and make it talk like you were born with it (and such shooters do exist), you need to shop for a gun that feels good in your fist and points like your finger.

Grip size and type affects how well you shoot a particular gun. Find one that fits your fist comfortably and points naturally. Most modern polymer pistols come with several sizes of grip inserts.

Most folks like the feel of 1911 pistols, and the way they fit your hand can be refined with grip panels of differing texture and thickness.

Most polymer-framed guns today have interchangeable grip inserts; find a model that feels good in your hand, and then refine that feel by finding the grip insert that fits your hand the best.

Most 1911 semiautos feel good to most folks, and feel can be somewhat refined through changing grip panels to slim width, or finding panels with a more or less aggressive texture.

As for revolvers, there are myriad aftermarket grips in wood, rubber, plastic, aluminum, stag, ivory, fake ivory, and so on. If you can't find a revolver grip that feels good to you, buy one that feels too big and get out the wood rasp.

◼ LONG BARRELS ARE MORE ACCURATE AND EASIER TO SHOOT.

I'm going to argue against extreme cases of this one. Long barreled guns do offer an increased sight radius, so aiming is more precise, but overly long barrels become whippy out on the business end. In other words, when quickly brought on target, they don't seem to become steady quite as fast. Imagine picking up a short length of 2x4 lumber and pointing it at a car across the street. Goes right to it, doesn't it? Now imagine picking up a 16-foot 2x4 and swinging it around to point at the car. You'll likely swing past it, back to it, and then wobble a bit before steadying on the car. Drastic example, I know, but it illustrates my point.

There is, of course, a middle ground. Extremely short barrels are even more challenging than extremely long ones. Popular semiauto barrel lengths are from four to five inches, and for good reason—they balance and maneuver well without being unwieldy. For revolvers, I really prefer a four-inch barrel unless I'm either concealing it, in which case I prefer a two- to three-inch barrel, or hunting with it, in which case I like a six- to eight-inch barrel.

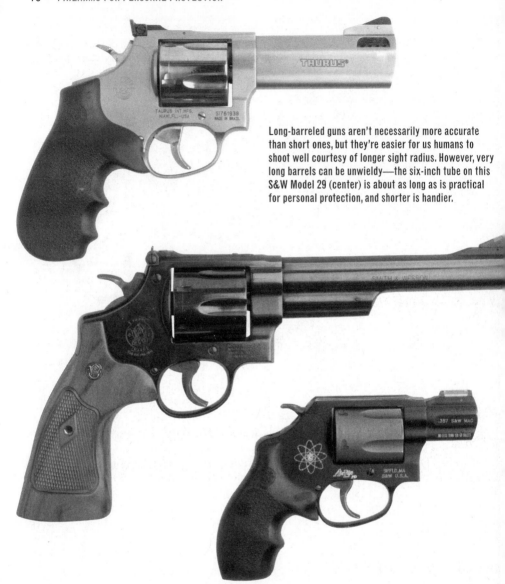

Long-barreled guns aren't necessarily more accurate than short ones, but they're easier for us humans to shoot well courtesy of longer sight radius. However, very long barrels can be unwieldy—the six-inch tube on this S&W Model 29 (center) is about as long as is practical for personal protection, and shorter is handier.

EXPERIENCE LEVELS DEFINE REALISTIC HANDGUN OPTIONS

No matter how much you enjoy watching Actress X blow through blanks in a brace of .50 AE Desert Eagle pistols, it just doesn't make sense to cripple your potential by choosing a handgun that is challenging to shoot. Frankly, most folks are best served with a standard-size semiauto in 9mm. Once you've mastered that, consider moving up to a .45 if you really think you need the extra authority. In revolvers, start with .38 Specials, and work up to .357 Magnums.

If you train consistently and build your skill and discipline enough, you can choose to shoot whatever model and caliber you darn well please. But by then, you'll be reading this book for recreation—if at all—because you will have gained the knowledge you need to make good choices in personal protection tools.

If you're going to carry it all day, every day, everywhere you go, you'll need something discrete but capable such as this compact S&W .38 revolver coming out of a Galco Meridian Holster Handbag.

If things ever get really, really bad because of a disaster—whatever it's nature—you just might want a big, no-nonsense handgun.

EXPECTED NEEDS AND HANDGUNS THAT MEET THEM

There are women out there whose biggest fear is that a hand will reach out from beneath their car and grab their ankle while they are unlocking the car door late in the evening in the mall parking lot. These ladies don't need a gun capable of defending a food stash from a gang of hungry bikers during the aftermath of a super volcano—they need a meat cleaver to detach the grabber's grabber. Since that is considered a bit uncivilized to many folks, a sleek, sophisticated, deadly little handgun seems more appropriate. Easily contained in the Dooney and Bourke, it will be inconspicuous until needed, and then rise to the occasion with aplomb.

I can't analyze every possible need and lay out a formula that will determine the perfect handgun for you. What I can tell you is to use your noggin.

Home defense is less of an issue to these gentlewomen than the concern of potentially having to scrape an unwanted suitor from their person while out and about. At home, there's likely an alarm system, or a big dog, or a gun-nutty husband. And while many of these women can make a full-size Glock tune up and sing if needed, they prefer—and need—a purse-appropriate compact gun instead. Like them, it behooves you to know your needs and choose appropriately.

Of course those anticipated needs can stretch the other way, too. Should you live in the sprawling suburbs of an accident-prone population center, you just might want something that will fend off a horde of hungry bikers. Or at least maintain their respect while you share food in trade for some fuel for your minivan. In that case, you definitely want something of authoritative appearance. Most any quality full-size handgun will do, though I've got to cast my vote for either a 1911 .45 Auto or a big revolver when it comes to authoritative appearance. That said, the gun in my go-bag is usually either a Glock 17 or a Smith & Wesson M&P9. Both are chambered in 9mm, both contain 17 rounds in the magazine. They are light-ish in weight, easy to shoot accurately, easy to shoot rapidly, and hold a bucketful of bullets.

I can't analyze every possible need and lay out a formula here that will help you determine the perfect handgun for your personal protection needs. What I can tell you is to use your noggin. Step back from "cool factor" when setting out to purchase a personal protection firearm. In fact, discard cool factor entirely. Considered objectively, you know what your real potential needs are. With a little research and some time drooling at the local gun shop, you can make a good decision. Just remember, in the personal protection realm, a gun is a tool. The better that tool is suited to your needs, the more you'll learn to trust it. And the more you trust it, the more effectively you'll use it.

CHAPTER 7:

HANDGUNS VS. RIFLES VS. SHOTGUNS

E ven military and law enforcement folks don't try to carry all three types of firearm—handgun, rifle, and shotgun—into harm's way. They are usually trained on all three, but even if you are Clint-Eastwood-tough, two is plenty to carry. And if you're an ordinary citizen going about his own business, one is hard enough.

So which is best? How does one decide between the three types and their vastly different capabilities and characteristics?

HANDGUNS

Handguns are light and easy to carry, concealable, very maneuverable, and easily brought into life-defending action with a minimum of effort. All of these attributes are valuable. Let's consider them separately.

You're more likely to have a light gun ready for action during a midnight search for a suspicious bump in the night than a heavy gun that fatigues muscles and tends to droop by your side. Taking that a step farther, a gun that is easy to carry is more likely to actually be with you when the naturally-produced fertilizer hits the fan than a gun that is bulky and unwieldy when strapped to your person.

Concealable guns offer two vital advantages: that of surprising the bad guy when you bring it into action, and that of being discrete enough to accompany you where any visible personal protection tool is inappropriate.

Being maneuverable is of greater importance inside buildings than outside. Inside, handguns are easier to "pie" around corners with than a long gun; they are easier to retain—meaning you are less likely to be disarmed because it's harder to for an attacker to grab and yank it away from you; they are easier for you to reverse directions with in case you're peeking down the wrong dark-and-scary hall, and so on. Outside, with space around you, you're far better off with a rifle.

A handgun carried on your person is the easiest of all cartridge-loaded lifesaving devices to bring into action, and even when kept in a nightstand or in your car's glove box, a handgun takes less effort to get to and fire than a long gun leaning in the bedroom corner or in your car's back seat or trunk.

On the flip side, handguns do have disadvantages, and when the danger is outside, those disadvantages can be significant. Handguns are far less accurate than a rifle, both

It's usually impractical to carry all three types of firearm—rifle, shotgun, and handgun—even in the most desperate circumstances. Figure out which best suits your needs and stick with one, or at most, two.

Though limited in range, handguns are maneuverable, discrete, and fairly capable. They're the most popular personal protection firearm type in America for good reason.

in inherent precision and in shootability. Past about 20 or 30 yards, a handgun rapidly becomes rather inept in a gunfight.

They are also less powerful than a rifle. There's a cliché saying that goes something like, "A handgun is only useful for fighting your way to your rifle." Rather narrow-visioned in my opinion, but in some contexts it has real value.

Pick a handgun as your preferred personal protection tool if you spend most of your time indoors, and if when outside you're in confined urban environments. Pick a handgun if you frequently go into situations where you've got to be discrete with your defense tool. Frankly, this description covers by far the largest demographic of humans today. The popularity of the handgun as a personal protection firearm is well placed.

Handguns have one additional incredibly powerful advantage: being so easy to carry, most folks carrying a rifle or shotgun can hang a handgun on their belt without feeling additionally encumbered, so it plays the part of a backup defense tool to perfection.

SHOTGUNS

Easily the second-most-popular type of personal protection firearm, shotguns are more powerful than a handgun, more forgiving in shot placement than a handgun, and rather intimidating if you are the unfortunately soul gazing down the gaping muzzle.

Shotgun pellets tend to over-penetrate less and lose velocity much faster than projectiles fired out of a handgun or, especially, a rifle, thus endangering fewer innocent bystanders. As a matter of neighborhood-preserving fact, typical shotgun pellets are

Even sporting shotguns are very effective personal protection tools.

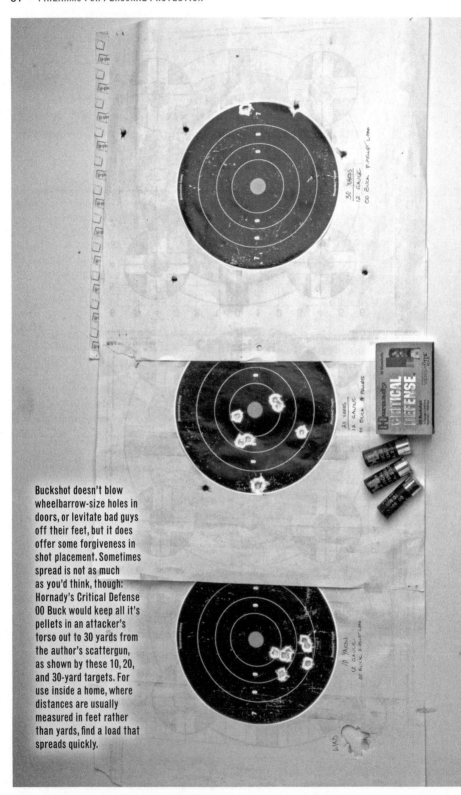

Buckshot doesn't blow wheelbarrow-size holes in doors, or levitate bad guys off their feet, but it does offer some forgiveness in shot placement. Sometimes spread is not as much as you'd think, though: Hornady's Critical Defense 00 Buck would keep all it's pellets in an attacker's torso out to 30 yards from the author's scattergun, as shown by these 10, 20, and 30-yard targets. For use inside a home, where distances are usually measured in feet rather than yards, find a load that spreads quickly.

incapable of flying farther than a few hundred yards. Bigger buckshot pellets go a bit farther, but not a lot. However, within ranges of about 30 or 40 yards, those pellets travel in a devastating cloud of evil-stopping lead.

> *Few indeed are the legitimate personal defense scenarios that would require you to shoot somebody 40 yards away.*

Because of the nature of that cloud of pellets, which opens up in a cone shape as it progresses farther and farther from the shotgun's muzzle, actually connecting with a violent attacker is easier than with a single projectile out of a handgun or rifle. You can catch the bad guy with an edge of the shot pattern and still turn his attitude instantly more peaceful.

Unlike Hollywood's dramatic depictions of the effect of a shotgun blast on the human body, bad guys won't levitate out of their boots and smash backward through the wall behind them. Nor are shotguns capable of cutting a two-foot-wide ragged hole through a door with a single shot. But a one-ounce load of lead pellets does hit remarkably hard, ending most life-endangering conflicts right then and there.

Shotgun enthusiasts tend to get all lathered up over the sound of a shotgun action—especially that of a pump-action—being racked. Shhhuck-CHUCK! Intruder's knees will wilt from beneath them, some folks claim, while the poor fellow begs for mercy, meanwhile wetting himself. Me, I'm not quite that enthusiastic, and I believe that the admittedly threatening sound of a shotgun action being functioned can sometimes be a disadvantage by giving away the position of the one holding it. But nobody, and I do mean nobody, likes gazing down the muzzle of a shotgun with an angry, frightened homeowner behind it.

Disadvantages of a shotgun? They are pretty ineffective past about 40 yards... but few indeed are the legitimate personal defense scenarios that would require you to shoot somebody that far away. You'd better have a really good argument to convince the jury that your life was actually in danger.

Shotguns are also somewhat unwieldy indoors, and can be grabbed and taken away from you more easily than a handgun. And they recoil pretty substantially, making it hard for recoil-sensitive and inexperienced shooters to get the best out of them.

Pairing a shotgun with a handgun makes less sense than pairing a rifle and a handgun. Though a shotgun is fearsomely powerfully and effective at close range, you're still limited to 40 yards or so. A handgun and a rifle combined offer both good close-range and indoor capabilities, and distance capability.

RIFLES

Rifles are less maneuverable, more powerful, and much, much more accurate, especially as distances stretch, than either a handgun or shotgun.

Now, some rifles are just not suitable for personal protection, for instance those of single-shot design. The best types for defense work are accurate, reliable semiautos that feed from high-capacity magazines, closely followed by lever-actions. You want the quick follow-up shot capability and ergonomic handling characteristics that these usually offer.

My personal favorites are the M1A (civilian version of the M14 military rifle), and the AR-15. Other good options are the legendary AK-47, the FAL, and the Mini-14. If you're a lever-gun guy, I really like quality pistol-caliber carbines in .357 Magnum and Winchester 1894s and Marlin 336 rifles in .30-30.

Rifles are less maneuverable, more powerful, and much, much more accurate, especially as distances stretch, than either a handgun or shotgun. This M1A Scout rifle is powerful, reliable, and carries 20 rounds of .30-caliber authority.

Undoubtedly the most popular personal-protection rifle in America, the AR-15 offers good maneuverability and accuracy coupled with low recoil.

While rifles are pretty effective at close ranges, they really come into their own as distances stretch. A good rifle will give you the ability to effectively hit targets of malicious intention out to 150 yards (with a lever-action or AK-47) and much, much farther with something like an M1A, FAL, or AR-15. Why you'd need to shoot somebody at that distance in order to preserve your own life is a tough question. Ordinary (if you could ever call a deadly confrontation ordinary) personal defense situations in today's world just don't happen at long range. However, Americans make being prepared a way of life, and if our country is ever (heaven forbid) invaded by a hostile power, or if we ever experience the breakdown of civilization, it's conceivable that we might find ourselves fighting for our lives or for the food and family that preserves our existence.

I'm not a doomsayer, but I never fault anyone for being prepared. Heck, I was a Boy Scout, and I do my best to be prepared myself.

Back to rifles. Many rifle calibers are so powerful that they actually become a liability in urban environments. Bullets will penetrate walls, cars, and even fat guys and just keep right on going, potentially endangering good folks in the neighborhood. On the other hand, in suburban areas, that downrange energy can be vital. Opening "personal protection" up to very broad interpretation, consider protecting one's livelihood—sheep, cattle—from predators, or feeding oneself if stranded in wilderness areas.

That's also where the much-greater accuracy provided by a rifle becomes important. A good rifle—in the hands of a good rifleman—will keep all of its shots inside a 1.5- or 2.0-inch group at 100 yards when fired from a steady rest, and a very accurate rifle will keep its shots inside a 1.0-inch group or even less. A magnified optic is usually necessary to achieve this level of accuracy, but not always—shooters skilled with iron sights rou-

Dominant worldwide; the AK-47 is a rugged, reliable fighting carbine. Despite it's many virtues, it's a bit limited in both accuracy and range.

tinely pull off very impressive shots. Just look at the service rifle divisions at the National Matches, which allow only iron-sighted rifles.

Though inherent accuracy is less of an issue within 40 yards or so, the ease of precise shot placement with a rifle—even in very stressful situations—gives it a distinct advantage for use in street-type or sprawling, slightly more open conditions.

Couple a good handgun with an AR-15 carbine or M1A Scout rifle, and you're well prepared to handle any life-threatening situation from spitting distance to some 300 yards. If, and it's a big if, you learn to use the rifle properly.

Ability is more about how well you use your chosen tool than it is about high capacity and gadgets. In the right hands, this lever action is a fearsome self-defense carbine.

RIFLE GALLERY

◼ AR-15 CARBINE

AR-15 Carbine

Probably the best crossover close-and-long-range rifle is the AR-15 carbine, which is moderately powerful, typically very accurate, compact enough to be maneuvered in dwellings or other city environments, and holds a plethora of ammo in detachable, easily changed lightweight aluminum or polymer magazines. Recoil is minimal, enabling very fast, on-target follow-up shots, and ammo is compact (as rifle ammo goes) and light, making it easy to carry plenty of extra rounds.

◼ M1A SCOUT RIFLE

M!A Scout

Another favorite (and the one I have the most personal affection for) is the M1A Scout rifle, which is a .308-caliber semiauto with 20-round steel magazines, built with a maneuverable 18-inch barrel. While not as accurate on average as an AR-15, they are plenty accurate enough for work out to 300 yards or so, and carry a lot more oomph. For those that prefer the legendary reliability of the M14-based action, the authority of the powerful .308 cartridge, and the look and feel of a pre-space-age rifle, it's impossible to beat.

◼ AK-47

Considered by many experts to be arguably the most robust, reliable, effective close-quarters fighting rifle in existence, the AK-47 shrugs off neglect, abuse, and the dirt and grit and fouling of very adverse environments. While it fires a relatively low-velocity cartridge (the 7.62x39mm) that lacks the ability to maintain steam as distances stretch, up close it carries devastating punch on the receiving end. Magazines generally hold 30 rounds, and are constructed of steel. Though very well built examples can be quite

AK-47

accurate, the primary fault of most AK's currently available in the U.S.A. is woefully inaccuracy. A good one will keep its shots in a 3.0- or 4.0-inch group at 100 yards, but most shoot groups of double or even triple that. However, inside of 100 yards, AKs are pretty darn hard to beat.

MINI-14

Ruger Mini-14

In essence a scaled-down, somewhat modified version of the legendary M14 battle rifle, Mini-14s are built by Ruger. Though typically chambered in .223 Remington, a few are available in 6.8 SPC (an intermediate semiauto rifle round slowly gaining popularity for close- to mid-range "tactical" use), and a variation called the Mini-30 shoots the 7.62x39mm (AK-47) round. Light, maneuverable, and typically very reliable, most Mini-14s suffer from sloppy tolerances and—as a result—usually aren't particularly accurate. Those of recent manufacture are said to be more consistent than older versions.

SCOUT RIFLES

Ruger Scout

Typically of bolt-action design, with the occasional semiauto sample such as the M1A mentioned above, a classic scout rifle has a shortish, maneuverable barrel with good iron sights; a box magazine offering high capacity; and a forward-mounted, low-magnification scope with very generous eye relief. Meant to be shot with both eyes open to enhance the shooters comprehension of what is happening around him and enable fast target acquisition, I personally think the forward-mounted scope is overrated but am in favor of all the rest.

For prepper types, who may believe that someday obtaining brass will be impossible, bolt actions trump semiautos because empty cartridge cases are easier to retain during ejection. When you're down to just a few carefully hoarded cases, that's a very real advantage.

■ FN FAL

FN FAL

While the United States were busy adopting the M14 rifle in the '50s, the rest of the NATO forces worldwide were testing and adopting the FN-built FAL. Definitely too heavy for really quick, responsive use, especially indoors, the FAL is a premium battle rifle for midrange use. Chambered for 7.62 NATO (.308 Winchester), it is a powerful rifle and—in good condition—is moderately accurate, making it well suited for close to mid-range use. Most magazines contain 20 rounds. Many available rifles are rebuilt surplus guns, though there are some civilian-legal versions in current production.

■ WINCHESTER 1892

Winchester Model 1892

Arguably the best of the lever-action pistol-caliber designs, the Model 92 is legendary for smooth feeding, reliable function, and quick handling. It's a very strong action, too, making it suitable for powerhouse cartridges such as the .44 Magnum, though as I've said elsewhere, for personal protection I'd choose one chambered in .357 Magnum. Effective range is limited to around 150 yards or so, and that only if you know your rifle well, but recoil is very light and the report (sound) is rather quiet in comparison to most rifles. Follow-up shots are a breeze, and standard carbines with 20-inch barrels usually hold 10 shots or more. Pair it with a good revolver in the same caliber for a simple self-defense system.

■ WINCHESTER 1894

Winchester Model 1894

With more than 7,000,000 rifles produced—more than any other one sporting rifle model in existence—the Model 94 is the real rifle that won the West. Most are chambered for the .30-30 cartridge, and ammunition is available in just about every gas station and corner hardware store across the nation. While it's still a short-range cartridge—200 yards on the outside—it's effective, both for feeding a family and protecting one. Most rifles hold six rounds and can't be reloaded particularly quickly, but are fast cycling, reliable, and the very soul of ergonomic.

◼ MARLIN 1894

Marlin Model 1894

Much like the Winchester 1892 in characteristics but more available, Marlin's handy little pistol-caliber carbine is a favorite by shooters in the cowboy action crowd—and they know a thing or two about choosing a lever gun that runs fast, smoothly, and reliably. Actions can be smoothed and tuned by a gunsmith to provide a greased-lightning feel, enabling a homeowner to make good use of the ten or so rounds of ammo in the magazine. Quick, maneuverable, and with excellent pointing characteristics, the Marlin 1894 is a sound choice for those desiring a lever-action rifle for personal protection.

◼ MARLIN 336

Marlin Model 336

Providing the only real challenge to Winchester's ubiquitous Model 94, the Marlin is a little less sleek in both looks and in the hand, but is—on average—perhaps just a shade more accurate. Also, since it has a true side ejection port, the top of the action is solid, making it more suitable—at least against early top-eject 94s—for mounting a scope. Robust and reliable, Marlins tend to generate great loyalty among shooters. For reloaders, it's worth knowing that most Model 336 rifles have Marlin's patented Micro-Groove rifling, which doesn't handle cast lead bullets well. It's best to stick to jacketed projectiles.

SHOTGUN GALLERY

There are many excellent self-defense shotguns on the market. As long as they are easy for you to function, robust, and completely reliable, you won't go wrong. I can't list all of them, obviously, but here are a few that I have personal experience with, trust completely, and can recommend without reservation.

■ REMINGTON 870 PUMP ACTION

Remington 870

No need to say "arguably" —the Remington 870 is without a doubt the most popular, proven combat and self-defense shotgun available. It's inexpensive and as reliable as an axe. There are many other good pump-action shotguns, but none even remotely approaches the 870 in reputation.

Available in myriad variations meant for everything from waterfowl hunting to military and law enforcement use, it's adaptable and easy to accessorize. The most popular and useful modifications to standard models are (1) a short, 18-inch barrel (less than 18 inches is illegal for a civilian to own) and (2) an extended magazine tube that increases ammo capacity from five rounds to seven.

Easier yet, just purchase an 870 variation already set up for personal protection right from the factory.

■ MOSSBERG 590A1 PUMP ACTION

Mossberg 590

Probably the second-best pump gun for personal protection, the Mossberg 590A1 differs from the more common Mossberg 500 mostly in the construction and material of small parts. For instance, most 500s have plastic safeties (Mossbergs have tang safeties, conveniently located for the thumb to flick them off in a split second), while 590A1s have metal safeties. Likewise several internal parts.

Not that the 500 is a bad shotgun—it's rather good for the price. But when purchasing a personal protection tool, spend the extra dollars for the 590. My personal favorite pump gun is in fact a highly customized Mossberg 500, but when the gunsmith worked it over he replaced all of the plastic parts, in effect making it a 590A1 with a tuned action and a high-tech finish.

Most 590A1s come with short barrels and extended magazine tubes, so usually no modifications are necessary to make them prime fighting tools. But like the Remington 870, myriad aftermarket accessories exist for Mossberg 500/590 series shotguns, and some of them are either useful or cool. Some aren't. The most useless has got to be vertical pistol grip buttstocks—any and all brands. Why? Because when shooting a gun with a vertical pistol grip stock, you've got to let go of the grip completely to engage and disengage the safety. You waste critical time (in which you could be made very dead very quickly); you reduce your control of your tool; and you may very well fumble the safety when under stress due to loss of fine motor skills. If you want a set of really good aftermarket stocks for your Mossberg 590A1 or 500, I recommend standard-profile Hogue Overmold stocks. That's what I use, and I love 'em.

BENELLI M2 TACTICAL

Benelli M2 Tactical

If you want a soft-recoiling defense shotgun, consider a semiauto. Benelli's M2 line is well reputed for reliability when it gets down and dirty, and is much-loved by hard-core 3-gun competitive shooters. They run their guns hard and put more rounds through in a season than most shooters do in a lifetime. M2s are extraordinarily robust, handle well, shoot well, and as long as you understand them, are very reliable.

What do I mean by "understand them"? Simply put, Benelli's may not go completely into battery (meaning the bolt is fully forward, locked, and in position to fire) if the shooter lowers the bolt gingerly — typically occurring when a fellow forgets whether his chamber is loaded and eases the bolt back for a peek, then lowers the bolt back into place. The bolt needs momentum to go into battery. The result of a bolt not fully in battery? A harmless "click" when the trigger is pulled. The good news is, the issue isn't hard to avoid, as long as you understand it. Don't lower the bolt softly; draw it back a ways and let it slam shut.

Almost all Benelli's—including the M2—are inertia driven, meaning that they harness recoil to function the semiautomatic action, rather than bleeding gasses off through a perforation in the barrel and harnessing it to function the action. As a result, they don't get the fouling buildup in the mechanisms that many competing shotguns do, which is nice if you don't like cleaning your guns.

The M2 is one of my all-time favorite personal protection shotguns. An even better recommendation is that the M2 Tactical is Payton Miller's (long-time executive editor of *Guns & Ammo* magazine) favorite defense shotgun. He shoots skeet with his—very successfully, I might add. M2s are a little costly—a lot costly compared to a Remington 870—but are worth every penny.

FN-USA SLP

FN-USA SLP

The first FN-USA shotgun I tested thoroughly was a rifled-barrel version of the versatile SLP. It was dead reliable, easy to function, and surprisingly ergonomic for a heavy hunk of fighting machine. Many competitive shooters are going to the award-winning FN SLP for those very characteristics.

Of gas-operated design, the SLP bleeds a tiny amount of propellant gasses off through a perforation in the barrel and harnesses it to function the action. Proponents of the design claim that it provides reliable function in a broad range of temperatures, ranging from very hot to very cold.

I don't own an SLP, but I'd like to. Every single SLP I've fired has left me newly impressed. They're very shooter-friendly and as tough as an anvil.

CHAPTER 8:

RIFLE CARTRIDGES AND SHOTGUN GAUGES

Discussing rifle cartridges for personal protection is an interesting business. With good expanding bullets, any caliber good for predator hunting or big game hunting is an effective bad-guy stopper. As is about any 20- or 12-gauge shotgun load. So choosing an effective cartridge kind of boils down to choosing a rifle you like. Choosing a good shotgun load is, well, pretty easy. Most any are good enough for defense at close quarters, and advantages between this load and that are slight and arguable. Don't worry, we'll argue 'em.

For the purposes of simplicity, only the classic cartridges typically chambered in rifle models legendary for personal protection and/or combat are discussed here. My apologies to loyalists of less common or obscure-but-capable cartridges not discussed here. As for shotgun loads, there are really only two gauges to discuss—12 and 20—along with a brief look at the upstart 410, for which recent R&D has produced some dedicated defense loads that are actually pretty impressive for such a pipsqueak hull.

Most centerfire rifle cartridges and shotshells work well for stopping a deadly threat as long as they're loaded with expanding bullets. Shown here, from left, is a lineup of cartridges commonly coupled with the best fighting guns: .223 Remington (aka 5.56 NATO), 6.8 SPC, 7.62x39mm, .30-30 Winchester, .308 Winchester (aka 7.62 NATO), 12 gauge, 20 gauge.

.223 Remington/5.56 NATO

.223 REMINGTON/5.56MM NATO
(AR-15, MINI-14 RIFLES)

First fielded aggressively in Viet Nam, the 5.56mm NATO cartridge rapidly gained a reputation for unreliable function and lackluster killing ability. Why? First, as I understand it, the cartridges sent to the troops in Viet Nam were loaded with a different, much dirtier powder than was originally spec'd and tested by military engineers, causing fouling issues for which solders were ill equipped and uneducated to overcome. Result: malfunctions. Lots of malfunctions.

In many cases, the 5.56 NATO cartridge penciled right through, leaving a knitting-needle hole through the enemy soldier—bad bullet karma when you need to drop the guy before he pincushions you with his rusty bayonet.

As for the lackluster killing ability, that is traceable to the original 55-grain Full Metal Jacket (FMJ) projectile designed for the 5.56. If it happened to "yaw" or tumble (destabilize and go end-over-end) on impact, especially if it broke into two or more pieces—usually at the crimping groove—as it tumbled, it did extensive damage and was very lethal.

However, in many cases it penciled right through, leaving a knitting-needle hole through the enemy soldier — bad bullet karma when you desperately need to drop the guy before he pincushions you with his rusty bayonet.

Ammunition has come a ways since then. The current load fielded by the military is the M855, featuring a 62-grain FMJ. It's a little better than the original 55-grainer, but in all honesty not much.

The loads used by current law enforcement departments and marketed for self-defense purposes are a much better choice. They don't meet the "humane" requirements of the Geneva Convention—far from it—but they impart devastating shock and trauma to the individual impacted.

All use expanding bullets of one description or another. Many of the very popular loads simply repurpose "varmint" bullets, which are designed to fragment dramatically on impact. The more sophisticated self-defense loads use "bonded" projectiles, with lead cores bonded to their copper jackets to minimize fragmentation while maintaining major expansion, and some use low-flash powders to minimize blindness incurred by muzzle flash when firing at night. Personally, I prefer the heavier range of bullets, from 60 grains up to 77 grains in weight. One great advantage of the .223/5.56mm is that the aforementioned varmint-type bullets tend to break up and disintegrate when passing through home walls, minimizing overpenetration and the resulting danger to family members and neighbors.

Lest I wax eloquent and ramble on, I'll just say this: the .223 is no buffalo stopper, but it's accurate; it recoils so politely that fast follow-up shots are possible, and it is light enough that carrying a large quantity of ammunition is feasible. It has its limitations, but after all the verbal lather and campfire groaning, it's actually a pretty good personal protection cartridge.

6.8 SPC

6.8 SPC (AR-15)

Though it is rapidly gaining popularity, I haven't jumped on the 6.8 SPC welcome wagon yet. Heralded as a replacement for the .223/5.56mm, it does offer more close-range punch, but lacks the aerodynamics to maintain its advantage as distances stretch.

I will say that many of the loads currently developed for the 6.8 SPC are ideal for personal defense. The military has not yet—that I'm aware of—adopted it in any form, so the focus has been on civilian use, and civilians want intruder-stoppers. As a result, many loads feature very effective expanding bullets, typically in the 110- to 120-grain range.

Though it recoils a bit more than the .223/5.56, it's still a pretty mild-mannered cartridge. It's really useful range maxes out at about 300 yards. Magazines hold about 30 percent less ammo than those for .223/5.56 cartridges.

7.62x39mm

7.62X39MM

Made legendary in the AK-47, the 7.62x39mm cartridge was actually designed during WWII and initially used in the RPD machine gun, then the SKS rifle.

Primarily a close-range proposition, it hits hard at close quarters but lacks the aerodynamics to maintain energy at longer distances. Recoil is noticeable but not entirely unpleasant. Until a few years ago, surplus ammunition was plentiful and cheap, and it can still occasionally be found in large quantities for those willing to pay.

The two 7.62x39mm rifles most suitable for personal protection are the AK-47 and the SKS. Due to the fact that most ammo is of FMJ design, and will penetrate several sets of the neighbor's walls before stopping, the 7.62x39mm is most suitable for use in rural environments.

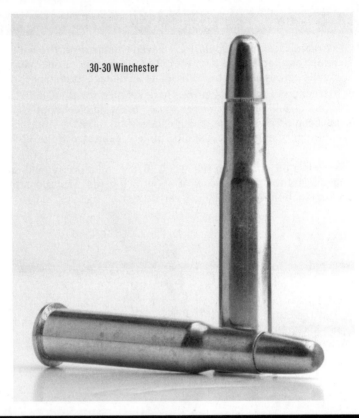

.30-30 Winchester

.30-30 WINCHESTER

An old warhorse that was never adopted as a common, prevalent military or law enforcement cartridge, the .30-30 nonetheless served capably in the hands of various law enforcement branches in the early part of the 20th century, and is a very effective self-defense round out to about 150 yards. Primarily available in lever-action rifles, it's not in the same realm as any of the good semiautomatic cartridges for hot and heavy combat, but for personal protection in an individual confrontation it does just fine.

The speed of follow-up shots is limited more by rifle design (lever-actions are slower than semiautos) than by recoil. Reloads are likewise slow—fresh rounds must be thumbed one at a time into the loading gate at the side of the action.

Most projectiles are in the neighborhood of 150 to 170 grains, and of flat- or round-nose design. Propelled at between 2,200 and 2,400 fps, their lackadaisical aerodynamics limit real effectiveness to about 150 or 200 yards.

In reality, .30-30 rifles are useful tools in rural settings, but are limited by overpenetration issues in densely populated urban areas. But that's rather fitting: classic lever actions helped win the West and are at home in country settings.

.308 REMINGTON/7.62X51MM NATO

Unless you are the sort that believes in the possibility of a major earthquake along the San Andreas fault, and wants a "get out of L.A." gun for when the city goes up in smoke and riots, you don't need a .308. However, for scenarios where real firepower—both in cartridge power and in rifle capacity—is the only thing that will keep your tail from getting permanently stuck in a crack, the .308 in an M1A Springfield Scout rifle is superb.

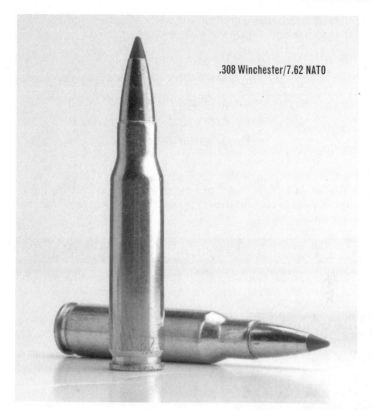

.308 Winchester/7.62 NATO

Obviously not your average personal protection cartridge, the .308, which is the civilian twin of NATO's 7.62x51mm round, is used by the military for mid-range sniping out to 800 yards or so. While outdated in terms of ballistics and aerodynamics when compared to modern high performers such as the 6.5 Creedmoor, the extraordinary popularity of the .308 makes it a good choice because ammo is common.

The .308 is considerably more powerful than the 7.62x39mm cartridge. Recoil is substantial but not prohibitive, making fast follow-up shots a matter of good shooting form and a correctly set up rifle. Magazine capacity is commonly 20 rounds, though 10-rounders are also common.

12 GAUGE

The legendary old 12-bore has been sweeping villains off of their black horses since the days they were loaded with loose powder, lead balls, and the occasional rusty nail and carried aboard horse-drawn coaches. It's as capable now—rather more so, as a matter of high-capacity fact—as it was then.

Current top-shelf personal protection loads are made up of eight or nine 00 buckshot, commonly known as "double-ought buck" over fairly light propellant changes, resulting in a cartridge that is a lovely combination of devastating on the downrange end and mild (as 12-gauge shotguns go) on the recoiling end. Double-ought buck is about .33 caliber, and though catching several of them at once tends to result in dramatic, instantaneous lead poisoning, they don't actually over-penetrate too badly. That's good in urban environments where endangering innocent neighbors is a very real concern.

Common "birdshot" loads—those using pellet sizes of #5s down to #8s—minimizes the overpenetration issue even further. Of only 0.09 to 0.12 diameter, such shot pellets come out in a cloud rather than a pattern, and while absolutely lethal at close ranges, the pellets tend to disperse and stop in walls as distances stretch.

> *The 410 was never a real contender in personal defense until some genius at Taurus Arms decided to make a revolver chambered for it.*

Shotguns that fire 12-gauge cartridges range from single-shots to legendary side-by-side double-barrel guns to state-of-the-art semiautomatic shotguns with extended-capacity tubular magazines.

20 GAUGE

Everything that can be said about the 12-gauge is more or less applicable to the 20-gauge, with the caveat that shotshell hulls hold a little less shot. This results in slight-

Few things are more fearsome personal protection tools than a robust, reliable 12-gauge pump-action shotgun.

From left: 12 gauge, 20 gauge, and 410 bore. With correct load choice, all are effective for personal protection.

ly less energy delivered downrange, but it's still plenty. A rather pleasant side effect is reduced recoil.

Literally dozens of various defense-appropriate loads exist for the 12 gauge. Not so the 20. They do exist, and in top-notch form, but they are fewer and harder to find.

410 GAUGE

The pipsqueak of the scattergun world, the 410 was never a real contender in personal defense until some genius at Taurus Arms decided to make a revolver chambered for it. At first the model was something of a flop. Then it was renamed the "Judge" and relaunched, along with the tale—accurate or not—that several judges in Florida were packing them into their courtrooms under their robes. Within a few years the Judge had become a household name.

Currently, most of the big-name ammo manufacturers offer dedicated 410 loads for personal protection. Some use buckshot, some use slugs, many use a combination of both. I'm not sure I buy into the concept wholeheartedly, but I do have to admit that a handgun loaded with a bunch of nasty lead pellets, discs, slugs, or buckshot makes it easier for a freaked-out, adrenaline-filled homeowner to connect on an intruder. I suppose my main beef with the concept is that it offers both limited capacity (most 410-bore handguns hold five rounds) and limited accuracy as distances stretch much past 30 feet.

This 410 shotshell hurls 3 plated disks and 12 1/4-ounce pellets.

CHAPTER 9:

PROFICIENCY AND SAFETY:

THE RESPONSIBILITY OF OWNING AND USING A GUN

I'll never forget the time that—as a 21-year-old hotshot shooter—I showed a new long-barreled Dan Wesson .357 Magnum revolver to the 14-year-old sister of a friend. It was an impressive piece. She asked to hold it. I confirmed that the cylinder was empty and handed it to her. She ogled it for a moment as my brother approached us, then turned and, grinning and gripping it with both hands playfully aimed it—to my surprise and horror—straight into his face from a distance of about 10 inches. Without an instant's hesitation he disarmed her quick as a wink, looked at us both like were the century's biggest idiots as he handed the revolver back to me, grip first, and said to her in a low voice that was so intense that she almost burst into tears, "Never, ever point a gun at me again."

It is the owner's responsibility to be sure that only people who deserve shooting get shot.

It is not enough to merely own a gun. A gun is a tool, a very dangerous tool, much like a power saw or a welder, and it is the owner's responsibility to be sure that only people who deserve shooting get shot.

Far too many people get the notion that they need a gun, waltz out and buy one, and smugly stow it away in their house, secure in the belief that they are now prepared for the worst. Nothing could be farther from the truth. Conditions like that lay the foundation for innocent humans, animals, and furniture to get shot.

Take a welder analogy: A neophyte with a powered-up welder and a stick of welding rod but no clue about how to use it is likely to blind and electrocute himself and everything else in the vicinity. A little basic knowledge and a healthy dose of common sense helps avoid catastrophe.

Difference is, welding is intimidating for first-timers. They seek help, and follow instructions. Not so first-time gun buyers, especially those of the masculine persuasion. Subconsciously guys think, "I Am Man. Therefore I Can Shoot."

It is not enough to merely own a gun. A gun is a tool, a very dangerous tool, much like a power saw or a welder, and it is the owner's responsibility to be sure that only people that deserve shooting get shot.

So what do you do to avoid being one of the armed and illogically dangerous? First, recognize that simply owning a firearm doesn't mean you are competent to use it either effectively or safely. Being humble goes a long, long way toward making you a responsible gun owner. Second, learn to use it. It's as simple as that.

What's the best way to become competent, safe, and proficient? There's no one simple answer. Read magazines and books. Ask for help from competent acquaintances (avoid gung-ho tactic-cool types) and be teachable. Practice. And it's well worth attending a reputable shooting school such as Gunsite Academy in Arizona. The instructors there will drum into you safe handling practices, sound foundational techniques, and will help you build good habits and achieve proficiency.

As a gun owner, it's your responsibility to be both proficient and safe. Study and research good techniques, and put in the practice time to make them second nature.

Attending a shooting course at a reputable shooting academy such as Gunsite can instill safety and teach you good handling, but it's still up to you to perfect that safety and skill through repetitive, quality practice.

This purpose of this book is not to teach combat drills and skills—we'll leave that to other books dedicated to the subject and to the capable instructors at the various schools. One word of caution when it comes to tactical shooting schools: Avoid pop-up schools run by over-aggressive, loud, self-aggrandizing "tactards." The best, most experienced gunhands are almost always easygoing and soft-spoken. They don't have to carry an abrasive attitude around to make themselves feel tough. They know what they can do, they've proven it in the field, and there's no use trumpeting it to an uncaring world.

10 COMMANDMENTS OF GUN SAFETY

The NRA (National Rifle Association) and other like-minded organizations have put together and adopted a list of gun safety "10 Commandments." They can be viewed online, at most gun clubhouses, in magazines, and whatnot, but they are sound and bear repeating. So here they are:

• Always keep the gun pointed in a safe direction.
• Always keep your finger off the trigger until ready to shoot.
• Always keep the gun unloaded until ready to use.
• Know your target and what is beyond.
• Know how to use the gun safely.
• Be sure the gun is safe to operate.
• Use only the correct ammunition for your gun.

- Wear eye and ear protection as appropriate.
- Never use alcohol or over-the-counter, prescription or other drugs before or while shooting.
- Store guns so they are not accessible to unauthorized persons.

The list varies a bit, but the content always addresses similar concepts.

Some of the items must be read with common sense. For instance, "Always keep your gun unloaded until ready to use." If you're carrying a gun for personal protection, you're using it. Keep it loaded. Don't get overzealous and wig out when a rule is interpreted differently than the way you see it.

Most critical on the list, in my opinion, is the first item—if you never allow the muzzle of your gun to point at something you're not willing to shoot, you'll never have a deadly accidental discharge. Deadly is the key word here—if you shoot and handle guns enough, you'll have one or more accidental discharges over the course of your lifetime, but with correct muzzle control the projectile will sail off harmlessly instead of killing, maiming, or damaging property.

"Sweeping" is probably the most common form of negligent muzzle control, and consists of waving a gun's muzzle across or past someone or something while transitioning from one position to another. It often happens when removing firearms from gun cases, when taking a slung rifle from your shoulder to bring it into shooting position, when loading and unloading guns into vehicles, when crossing fences, and so on. The only way to completely overcome it is to build a high level of awareness and create habits of detouring the muzzle around anything you wouldn't want to shoot.

There is simply no excuse for distracted or negligent gun handling—that's how people get shot. If somebody "sweeps" you with his muzzle, kindly but firmly tell him not to. If it happens again, it's ok to get irate.

Having a gun's muzzle negligently pointed at me is something that turns my blood cold. I simply won't tolerate it. If the handler is careless enough to let it wander in my direction, he or she is careless enough to perhaps have a round in the chamber, and careless enough to absently stroke the trigger. Combine the three and you've got a dead me—something I disfavor strongly.

If I get covered by a gun muzzle while out shooting or hunting, I tend to quietly but firmly remind the individual holding it not to do that, trying to avoid embarrassing him or her. If it occurs again I tend to get slightly irate. A third time makes my skin crawl and I get as far away from the careless shooter as I can.

Two other very critical gun handling practices are trigger-finger control—always keeping the trigger finger away from the trigger until ready to fire—and keeping your guns out of reach of those likely to cause an accident with them. While that usually means children, it can include your best friend's innocent fiancé or your senile grandmother, too. Recognize that if a little kid picks up your gun—one that you've carelessly left out on a table, loaded, and shoots his baby sister in the head, you are just as responsible as he is. Rather more so, in fact. Accept responsibility and keep your guns out of reach of those likely to misuse them.

Reloading under the stress of a life-or-death situation is hard. Learn correct technique and practice until the motions are ingrained into your muscle memory.

Good trigger control is not easy to master, especially with heavy recoiling handguns. Disciplined practice is required.

PROFICIENCY

Like driving a car, proficiency comes through extended, focused use. In the case of firearms that can be broken down into three areas of proficiency: gun handling and manipulating skills (loading, functioning the action, drawing, unloading, and so on); actual shooting skills (achieving a strong, steady position, aiming properly, squeezing the trigger, following through); and maintenance (field stripping, cleaning, and so on).

Squeezing a trigger is about the simplest of the shooting concepts to grasp and the hardest to master.

Handling and manipulating skills take time to polish. Any Neanderthal can fumble his way through getting a firearm loaded, chambering a round, and firing, but that kind of gun handling will get you mincemeated when the friendly neighborhood child molester pays your family a midnight call. Learn the correct way to load your gun's magazine or cylinder, to chamber a cartridge, holster and draw, and to safely unload and clear the gun when it's time to put it away. Then practice those skills until they become embedded into your muscle memory.

Making accurate shots requires both correct foundational skills and discipline. Foundation skills can be acquired through correct practice under the tutelage of an accomplished shooter, or through reading and Internet research. Learn correct shooting position, correct sight picture, and how to squeeze a trigger.

Squeezing a trigger is about the simplest of the shooting concepts to grasp and the hardest to master. A gun's sight absolutely must remain on the intended target as the trig-

ger "breaks," while the firing pin travels forward and impacts the primer, while the impact-sensitive priming compound ignites and flashes flame into the propellant, and while the bullet travels down the barrel. Though all this only takes milliseconds, any movement is too much movement. So when squeezing a trigger, the only thing that should move is your trigger finger—minimally—and the mechanical parts of the gun. Follow-through is vital.

The trouble is, when a gun fires in one's hands, one is in essence holding a contained, controlled explosion. The gun emits a loud bang and kicks like a possessed mule. Human bodies don't like that. Our minds can force our fingers to pull triggers, but the tendency is to anticipate the recoil and tense against it, often anticipating the shot and pushing into the expected recoil.

ABOVE: Small, powerful guns such as this Ruger snubnosed .357 Magnum recoil aggressively. It's a challenge to hold it perfectly still and squeeze the trigger without tensing and jerking.

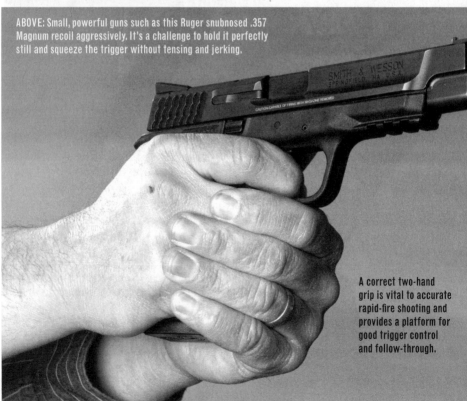

A correct two-hand grip is vital to accurate rapid-fire shooting and provides a platform for good trigger control and follow-through.

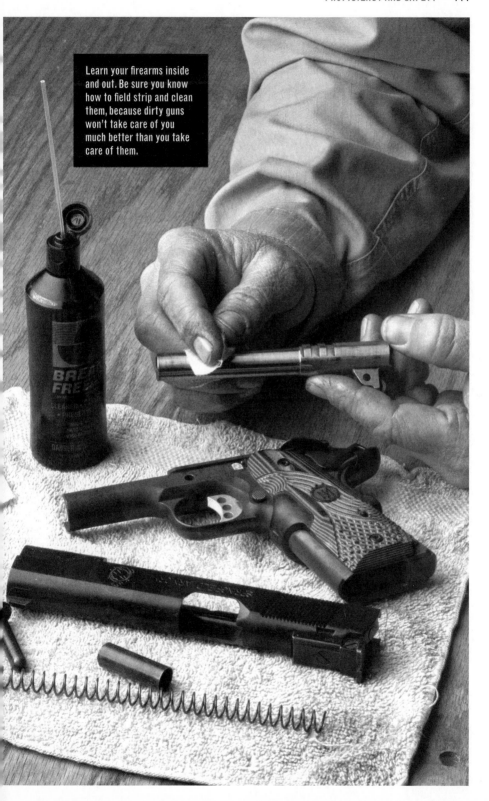

Learn your firearms inside and out. Be sure you know how to field strip and clean them, because dirty guns won't take care of you much better than you take care of them.

Shooting steel plates against a timer is a good way to polish your target acquisition, trigger control, and recoil control skills. The grey streak in the middle of the photo is the bullet, headed for the plate just to the left of it. Note the strong, correct grip and the resulting minimal muzzle jump.

For slow shots where precision is paramount, squeezing the trigger—slowly increasing pressure until the trigger breaks—is critical. When correctly squeezing a trigger, you won't know exactly when the gun will fire. You know it will go in the next few seconds, but there's no "NOW" feeling.

When shooting rapid-fire, there's obviously no time to squeeze slowly and let the shot surprise your reflexes. You've got to maintain an iron grip, following through each shot, and press the trigger. Don't slap it, don't jerk it—press it.

Easier said than done. Every good shooter I know has gone through a stage in their career where they battled a flinch—frequently a massive one. The shooters that battle through it and develop the mental discipline necessary to squeeze a trigger cleanly and correctly are the ones who become great. Far, far more common are the shooters who end up in an endless, ongoing vicious circle of flinching. Don't be one of them.

One of the most effective flinch-breaking tools is a revolver. Many shooters don't believe they are flinching, and when dry firing an empty gun they don't flinch. Load two or three random cylinder chambers in the revolver, hand them the gun, and watch them flinch when the hammer falls on the empty chambers. I've seen semi-experienced shooters flinch so hard that they became thoroughly embarrassed. Embarrassment is a strong motivator.

But I've digressed long enough. Last in the proficiency triad is firearm maintenance. Quality guns run astonishingly well with very little care, but that doesn't give you a free ticket to laziness. Learn to field strip your guns (new guns come with a manual containing instructions, and manuals can be downloaded for most popular models should you purchase a used gun without the manual). Learn to properly clean your firearms, and purchase the correct equipment to do so. Learn to reassemble them correctly. I've seen many a gun refuse to function because it was put together slightly incorrectly. And it doesn't hurt to learn to take your guns apart and put them back together under pressure, either. You may someday have to perform a field diagnosis on a gun that's gone belly up at the worst possible time.

Chapter 14 addresses correct cleaning methods and maintenance, and chapters 11, 12, and 13 cover the fine points of setting up your gun to get the best out of it. For now, suffice it to say that extensive, correct handling, focused dry-fire practice, and frequent maintenance—whether your gun needs it or not—is a good way to build the skills and muscle memory you need to be a safe, responsible gun owner.

CHAPTER 10:

THE PRACTICAL/ TACTICAL DICHOTOMY
(DON'T LET ATTITUDE OVERTAKE COMMON SENSE)

"Tactical"—a buzzword now so commonplace as to no longer have any real meaning—has become popular. Seems like some shooters can no longer even go to the range without suiting up in tactical pants with strategically located pockets, a tactical vest laden with techy tactical gear, tactical holsters and "drag bag" tactical rifle cases, and a whole bunch of tactical attitude.

You can no more put on tactical togs and attitude and magically become SWAT-team capable as a shooter than you can buy a cowboy hat, Wrangler jeans, and a nice pair of boots and transform instantly into a working cattleman.

I recently sat at a shooting bench at a public rifle range, and listened in amazement to the two shooters at the benches to my left. One was shooting an expensive precision rifle, the other peered through a spotting scope at a downrange target. Sporting the pale skin and plush personal upholstery of indoor desk jobs with too many free donuts, they were clearly anything but genuine tactical, despite their BLACKHAWK! and 5.11 garb. Still, they went through the routine with astonishing intensity. The guy glaring into the spotting scope would tersely spit out, "Spotter ready!" The reply would come grinding back, "Shooter ready!" Without even a pause to confirm wind conditions, wannabe number one would echo, "Send it!" and the guy with the rifle would fire. Somewhere not far downrange a steel gong would ring. Sometimes they repeated the whole routine over, and over, and over. Every single shot.

You don't need to dress in tactical clothing with enough pockets to hide a Christmas tree and all the trimmings to be effective with a gun. Know your tools and use them with skill, but don't change your style and attitude just because you carry a gun.

What a waste of energy, I thought as I screwed my earplugs in deeper and placidly continued firing test groups with whatever handload I was working up at the time. It's one thing for a professional sniper team or serious competitive team to practice working together on wind calls and shot placement, under tricky shooting conditions. It's even good to work together with a friend spotting for you when practicing at extended distances with your hunting rifle. But I'll tell you what: those two guys had watched too many movies, or perhaps attended too many classes run by a hot-shot tactical instructor who cussed at them like a real drill sergeant and made them feel tough.

TACTICAL TOGS DON'T MAKE YOU TOUGH

Tough is inside, not a shell you wear so people can see it. Especially when you are carrying a gun. Competence is something you don't have to prove, and those who really are competent never try to. When guns are involved, good judgment and common sense are far greater assets than a tough attitude. And you can't put on ability with a pair of tactical trousers, no matter how expensive they are.

One of the most dangerous men I know is a retired P.I. who worked Detroit. He has a disarming, engaging demeanor, and wears Hawaiian shirts, loose jeans, and loafers religiously. Another looks like a librarian, but can wield a vintage sniper rifle better than the Russians that built them. And I know middle-aged cowboys that can shoot the head off of a rattlesnake with a pistol or pick off a running coyote at 150 yards with a bolt-action rifle, but they wear stained straw cowboy hats, loose Wranglers over their flat asses, and Carhartt jackets.

Practical competition such as 3-gun shooting is a great way to polish your ability to shoot well under stress.

Rural dwellers often use their firearms in defense of home and garden—from destructive furry critters—and become comfortable and capable with them as a result.

My point is this: don't make the mistake of assuming that dressing the "tactical" part will gain you respect or authority; and don't disrespect true tactical gear by flaunting it around the local range, Olive Garden, or cinema. The guys that stuff was designed for—our boys in the trenches overseas and in Miami, Detroit, New Orleans, and so on—use it hard and sometimes the success of their mission depends on it. But you watch, when those guys show up at the range or a shooting competition they're likely in shorts and a tee shirt. Probably a tight tee shirt to show off the physique that their chosen lifestyle has built. But still, they leave the serious gear for when it's needed. So should you.

Now, I'm not saying you shouldn't own a tactical vest, combat boots, and a frikkin' cavalry saber if you want it. I do. If natural disasters, financial collapse, or invasion by a hostile

Wandering afield with a light-caliber handgun and plinking at targets of opportunity helps you learn to adapt to different situations.

government ever cause the breakdown of civilization, you may want and even need that gear. Just don't wear it around as if you live your life in it, and most of all, don't expect that simply by donning a bunch of tactical clothing an aura of natural skill, ability, and authority will somehow distill upon your person. Likely, all you'll look is slightly awkward.

Fit your guns to your lifestyle. Wear what is natural to you and what you are comfortable in. Don't change your manner of dressing and acting just because you've got guns.

One last note: wearing tactical gear marks you. Those with criminal intent know cop clothes, and they know when a cop is wearing them, and when a guy wearing them isn't a cop. Anywhere that concealed carry is legal, tactical garb screams "gun!" to those around you. Personally, when I'm carrying a gun I don't want the crowd to know it. I want to maintain the element of surprise, and I want to avoid the scrutiny of law enforcement who watch for armed attitudinal personalities.

KEEP IT PRACTICAL, NOT TACTICAL

Okay, I got hung up a bit on clothing and gear, because it's the outward manifestation of an internal attitude. However, the real root of the pseudo-tactical evil infesting a number of otherwise decent shooters comes from too much attitude-affecting cool factor.

Across America, the orientation of shooters has changed from hunting and traditional sport shooting to tactical shooting. Just observe the burgeoning popularity of 3-gun shooting, precision rifles, tactical carbines, and so on. In and of itself, it's a great thing. I can't say conclusively what's caused it, but seemingly it's a byproduct of all the troops that have served our country over in Iraq and Afghanistan over the past decade or two. When they come home, those who appreciate firearms purchase civilian-legal guns similar to the ones they carried in combat. They enjoy and promote the type of shooting that challenges those firearms.

Most of them didn't grow up hunting and shooting for practical reasons. Few indeed are those who have bumped off a skunk with a single-shot 12 gauge or wandered through frosty November woods in search of deer. Yesteryear's shooters were perhaps less cutting-edge, but they were far more practical because to them a firearm was a tool. They protected livestock, filled the larder, and yes, protected themselves and their families with those tools.

Today, few shooters actually use their firearms for honestly practical purposes. Let me qualify that. Personal protection firearms could be said to be continually in use, in an on-call sort of capacity, though we hope and pray that we'll never have to make that call. What I mean by saying that few shooters actually use their gun in a practical sense is that, well, protecting the cabbage patch isn't exactly something many of us do these days. As a result, firearms have morphed from being tools into being recreational instruments in the minds of many.

I'm all for using firearms for recreational purposes. I do so personally and attempt to promote doing so with every opportunity. But I also attempt to instill in neophyte shooters a sense of respect and responsibility that enables and protects the fun they're having.

Interestingly, there's a fundamental difference in gun-using rural folks, especially those with farms, livestock, or large gardens. Bluntly put, they've killed. Often, in the case of those with large flocks of sheep, or poultry, or—as in the case of Mr. McGregor of Peter Rabbit fame—cabbage patches: they've killed often. Although many of them are passionate hunters, much of that killing has been out of necessity, occurring while protecting their income and thereby their way of life.

> *Anywhere that concealed carry*
> *is legal, tactical garb screams "gun!"*
> *to those around you.*

Considered in that light—wherein the agricultural assets that support a way of life are protected from predators—one could say that rural folks actually employ guns in "personal protection" circumstances rather regularly. Whether those folks are an elderly couple weeding marauding rabbits out of their lettuce in southern Arizona, or an Alaska stockman shooting wolves out of his calves, they're employing their firearms for real purposes. They are killing. They know what it means to draw a bead on a living, breathing rib cage and squeeze a trigger. Use—real use—breeds respect.

Hunters, whether meat hunters or trophy hunters or, as is the case most of the time, a combination of the two, usually have similar experience to their credit. They've felt the extraordinary pressure of attempting to make a difficult shot under tricky circumstances. They've succeeded, and watched the life ebb from bodies, and they've failed, and watched their families go short of winter meat.

Though nothing can or should prepare the human mind for deliberately shooting to kill another human being, these folks—these farmers, gardeners, livestockmen, and hunters—have a better understanding of firearms, of their function as takers and providers of life, than do their urban counterparts. Don't take me wrong—I'm not saying that it's good or bad. I'm saying that there's simply less understanding present where guns are rarely put to use for practical purposes.

Pursue practical ability in firearms, as opposed to tactical ability. While being obsessed with perfecting the five-step draw is well and good, it's better yet to emulate your ancestors who lived with firearms as constant companions. Work on safety first, until keeping your finger off the trigger and your muzzle well controlled becomes pure muscle memory. Then work on proficiency, becoming so comfortable with your chosen firearms that loading and manipulating them is subconscious, allowing you to focus all your attention on any scenario unfolding around you, and to making a good shot should the situation deteriorate to that point.

If you like clean, low-cholesterol meat and spending time afield, put your personal protection tools to good use supplying the dinner table. Doing so will polish skills and teach you to shoot well under stress.

Look at the world through different eyes. Don't report the dusty grade school kid trudging down the shoulder of the street with a bloody squirrel in one hand and a .22 rifle in the other—smile at him. If he needs help carrying that .22 safely, help him briefly and with positive encouragement. If not, keep your mouth shut—he probably knows more about guns than you do.

Carry your guns with mild intent. As a citizen, you're not being called upon to hold the tactical edge that will assist you in enforcing laws and upholding truth and justice. Your responsibility as a gun owner is to yourself and your family. Become good with your guns, and discrete with them as well. Show up at the local 3-gun shoot in shorts and a Hawaiian shirt, or Wranglers and cowboy boots. Always remember, it's not about what you use, it's how you use it.

Firearms kept the first settlers in the New World alive. They won our forefathers a nation of freedom. They've protected that freedom through numerous wars around the world, and they've fed and protected American families for centuries. Firearms are the primary tool of American independence.

That, my friends, demands respect and good, practical, common sense. Wear your guns comfortably, like a well-worn wristwatch, not pretentiously. Shoot them capably, like you drive your favorite car, not with swagger. Handle them easily, like an extension of your body, not with flamboyancy. And use them to protect life, not to take it, even if the end result is the same.

CHAPTER 11:

GET THE MOST OUT OF YOUR HANDGUN

Handguns are probably the most popular of all firearms, and are certainly the most difficult to shoot well. Though this book is not intended to teach advanced skills, drills, and techniques with each and every firearm type suitable for personal protection (it would take a set of volumes that would do the Encyclopedia Britannica credit to accomplish that), there are certain foundational principles of setting up a firearm for consistent, accurate shooting, along with building personal skills that get the most out of that firearm, that are worth addressing.

Although incredibly versatile, handguns are not particularly easy to shoot well. Without correct foundational skills you'll struggle to get the best out of your sidearm.

Building a correct position enables you to hold your handgun steady for accurate shooting and control recoil for fast follow-up shots.

THE PERFORMANCE TRIAD

Good shooting is like a tripod: it takes three legs, or skill sets. I think of those legs as a performance triad. Without all three skill sets present and accounted for, accuracy goes AWOL.

The three are position, sight alignment, and trigger control.

The first leg is position, which, in the case of handgun shooting, covers stance, grip, and shooting in supported positions. Why is position first? Because without a correct, stable position, neither of the other two legs of the performance triad can be accomplished.

Correct sight alignment is crucial to consistently accurate shooting. When you aim, be sure that the front sight is centered in the rear notch, and that the top of both sights is perfectly parallel.

Position is important because position is what lends stability to the firearm. No matter how perfect your sight alignment is, and how much trigger control you have, you can't consistently hit a target if your position doesn't prevent your gun from waving around like a drunk witch's wand. Build a good, stable position, and you'll find that mastering sight alignment and trigger control are much easier.

Sight alignment is important because (1) if your sights are not regulated to place your bullet's impact on target and (2) you are personally incapable of lining them up exactly the same way for each

Once you've built a steady position and achieved a good sight picture on your target, the ability to press the trigger without jarring the sights off target is vital to good shot placement.

and every shot, you'll never be able to predictably and consistently hit your target. Master sight alignment, pair it with a good position and excellent trigger control, and you will not only be able to hit your target predictably, you'll be able to place your shots exactly where you want them on that target.

Trigger control is important because no matter how steady your position is, and no matter how perfectly and consistently you line up the sights, if you jerk the trigger and rattle the whole ensemble as the gun fires, hitting a target at all—let alone precisely—becomes purely a matter of luck. Trigger control is the third skill on this list, but do not be fooled: it is also the apex. It's where all the others focus and come to fruition. Good trigger control is absolutely vital to good shooting.

Here's a breakdown of each skill set, as it applies to handgun shooting.

POSITION (STANCE, GRIP, SUPPORTED POSITIONS)

Getting your stance right while shooting a handgun defensively is important for two reasons. The obvious reason is so that you can hold your handgun steady and get off a good, accurate shot. Perhaps more importantly when you are fighting for your life, your stance needs to help you absorb and control the recoil of several shots in rapid succession without getting put off balance.

For several decades, the "Weaver" stance, as taught by Jeff Cooper, was considered the best for fast, combat-type shooting. Currently the "modern Isosceles" stance has gained popularity and is being used by most of the very good action-pistol competitive crowd, which is a pretty good indication that it best supports fast, accurate shooting. Though I grew up using the Weaver stance, I've come to prefer the modern Isosceles. Lots of very good shooters use some adaptation of one or both. I think what stance will serve you best depends on your physique, hand and arm strength, sense of balance, and numerous other elements.

In essence, the Weaver stance is taken with a push-pull grip: your gun hand pushes toward the target, into a cup created by your weak hand, which pulls back toward the body,

LEFT: The Weaver stance shown here has been successfully used by combat shooters for many years, although most of today's best action shooters now use the Isosceles or modified Isosceles stance. To built a good Weaver stance, stand with your feet shoulder width apart, left foot (for right-hand shooters) leading. Cradle the gun with a push-pull grip, the left hand pulling rearward and the right pushing forward into it. The left elbow should be low, the right arm only slightly bent.

RIGHT: Very fast rapid fire is possible with a correctly built Isosceles stance. Place your feet shoulder width apart and almost square to the target, weight on the balls of the feet, clench the gun hard, roll your shoulders up toward your ears, and extend your arms almost straight. While uncomfortable at first, a good Isosceles position turns your whole body into a recoil spring, enabling you to control recoil very effectively.

OPPOSITE RIGHT: Whatever position you use, with whatever firearm, keeping your weight forward on the balls of your feet is vital to controlling recoil for fast follow-up shots.

creating opposing forces that enable very steady aiming. Keep the strong-hand elbow almost straight, and the support elbow bent and pointing almost straight down. The left foot should be forward (for right-hand shooters) of the right, in a boxing-like stance. Keep the bulk of your weight on the balls of your feet.

The modern Isosceles stance feels more awkward at first, and is harder to

Grip your gun high, keeping muzzle jump to a minimum.

A sloppy, low grip allows a gun to leap in your fist during recoil, drastically inhibiting your ability to shoot fast and accurately.

There are many variations of grip, but perhaps the most useful is to clench the gun hard with both hands, both thumbs extended down the side of the frame and slide. The harder you grip it the less it jumps, the quicker it returns to target, and the harder it is for you to flinch off target during rapid fire.

become comfortable with, but once it's engrained into muscle memory it's incredibly effective. Your hands should clamshell the gun, both elbows slightly bent, shoulders rolled up toward the ears. Feet should be shoulder width apart and almost side by side—the left may be a few inches forward if desired to help avoid getting set back on the heels during recoil. However, keep 70 percent of your weight on the balls of your feet, knees bent, shoulder weight ahead of the hips, head ahead of the shoulders, and you won't get rocked back by the biggest hand-cannon in this beautiful land. The great advantage of this position is that your entire body acts as a shock absorber, making very, very fast, accurate rapid-fire shooting possible.

Try both. The Weaver stance will be more comfortable at first, but try both. Eventually you'll find some variation that suits you and your physique. And if you don't remember anything else but this, keep your weight forward on the balls of your feet.

If your stance is your foundation, your grip is like the lag bolts that keep your house from getting wobbly when the tempests blow. I once overheard Ed Brown—one-time top competitor and current world-class pistolsmith—asked how hard one should grip a handgun. "Oh, about until the blood starts to drip," was his reply.

Like loose bolts, a loose grip makes for a sloppy, jumpy gun in your grasp—one that is hard to control during recoil and impossible to shoot rapidly and accurately.

When gripping a semiauto pistol, get a grasp high on the grip, with the web between your thumb and forefinger pressed firmly up into the curve where the grip frame comes back over the top of your fist. This helps control recoil. Make sure the barrel is lined up with your forearm, so it will transfer recoil straight up your arm (instead of out through the base of your thumb).

Now add the support hand, wrapping all four fingers over the top of your other fingers. Keep them below the trigger guard. Lay your support-hand thumb straight down the side of the frame just below the slide. The heel of your support hand should fit firmly and snugly against the heel of your strong hand, and the strong-hand thumb should lay straight forward along the top of the base of the support-hand thumb. Now, grip hard. Squeeze just short of the point where your hands tremble with tension.

Keeping the two thumbs stacked and both pointing straight forward down the side of the gun is tricky, and you'll have to pause and reset them frequently at first, but their position is very important. Press the support thumb hard into the side of the frame. Correct thumb position helps a gun point naturally and come on target more quickly and more naturally, helps index your grip for consistency, and—believe it or not—helps control recoil.

> *When shooting single-action, use the support-hand thumb to ear the hammer back, not the gun-hand thumb.*

Gripping a double-action revolver is similar. Again, get your gun-hand grasp up as high as possible on the stock, and make sure the barrel is lined up with the forearm. Wrap

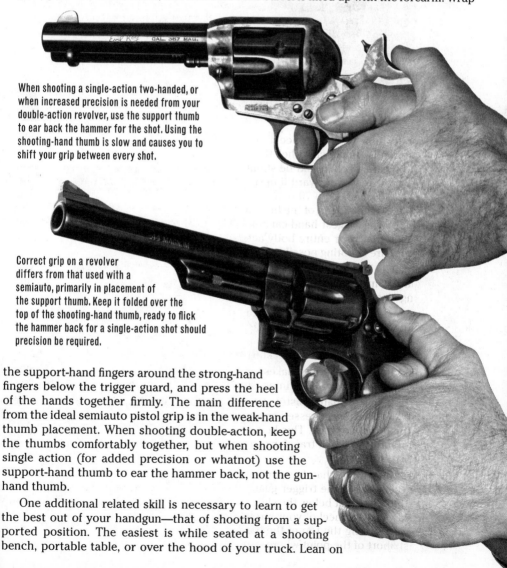

When shooting a single-action two-handed, or when increased precision is needed from your double-action revolver, use the support thumb to ear back the hammer for the shot. Using the shooting-hand thumb is slow and causes you to shift your grip between every shot.

Correct grip on a revolver differs from that used with a semiauto, primarily in placement of the support thumb. Keep it folded over the top of the shooting-hand thumb, ready to flick the hammer back for a single-action shot should precision be required.

the support-hand fingers around the strong-hand fingers below the trigger guard, and press the heel of the hands together firmly. The main difference from the ideal semiauto pistol grip is in the weak-hand thumb placement. When shooting double-action, keep the thumbs comfortably together, but when shooting single action (for added precision or whatnot) use the support-hand thumb to ear the hammer back, not the gun-hand thumb.

One additional related skill is necessary to learn to get the best out of your handgun—that of shooting from a supported position. The easiest is while seated at a shooting bench, portable table, or over the hood of your truck. Lean on the bench with your chest, minimizing body movement, and rest your handgun over a sandbag. If you don't want to purchase a sandbag at the local gun shop, you can make one by filling the cutoff leg of a pair of old jeans with clean sand and tying off both ends. Rest both elbows on the bench, and relax into a hunched-forward position to shoot. This position, correctly built, enables you to hold your handgun perfectly, absolutely steady, which makes achieving correct sight alignment and a clean trigger squeeze much easier.

This is how I accuracy-test all my handguns, and it's vital to ascertaining what load shoots the best from your particular gun, and finding its point of impact at 15 to 25 yards.

Finally, you'll want to practice and become comfortable with improvised field positions. Find a remote place where you can shoot without disturbing the neighbors, and wander with your handgun. A rimfire is perfect, if you've got one, because of the quiet report and cheap ammo. Practice leaning against trees, over the top of stumps, rocks, or fence posts, and sitting down with your heels planted and your knees up to support your arms as you aim. With a bit of trial and error, you'll find field positions that enable you to make quite difficult shots at surprising distances.

No, this is not the sort of shooting you'll do if ever placed in a kill-or-be-killed situation. In today's world, that type of shooting only typically happens to civilians up very close and personal. But this is worth considering: Even in very close gunfights, most people—police included—miss most of their shots. Why? Multiple reasons, including blindly shooting in a panic, but one of the biggest causes, in my opinion, is that they never mastered accurate shooting in the first place.

I have no doubt at all that—even with shocking amounts of fear-induced adrenaline coursing through your veins—honest skill serves you well in deadly encounters. Muscle memory is muscle memory, and if you've built refined skills into those sinews of yours, that skill will serve you well when you've got to stop the bad guy right now, before he kills you or someone you love.

SIGHT ALIGNMENT

Unless your sights are aligned exactly the same, in relation to each other and to the target every time you shoot, the impact of your bullets will be erratic and unpredictable.

Using an optic minimizes potential sighting variation, but few personal protection handguns utilize an optic. They tend to be fragile and bulky—neither of which are desirable traits in a tool that has to remain reliable and accessible through thick and thin. Learning to get the best out of iron sights is worth doing.

Most handgun sights consist of a square-topped "post" front sight, and a flat-topped rear with a square notch. When engineered correctly, the rear notch is just wide enough that when viewed at arm's length there's a bit of space on each side of the front sight. Key to consistency is to have the flat top of the front sight even with the flat top of the rear sight, and equal space on each side of the front.

Equal in importance is where to hold the sights on the target. Ideally, your point of impact at about 15 to 25 yards should be exactly at the top center of the flat-topped front sight. If your target is a paper plate at 25 yards, with a thumb tack in the middle holding it to the target backing, you'll halve the target with your front sight, putting the tack right on the top of your front sight, even though at that distance it will appear like a speck of dust on the flat plane that is the top of the sight. If you hit the tack consistently, quit your job and join the professional competitive shooting circuit. Realistically, you're just striving to put your bullets into a nice tight cluster in the middle of the paper plate.

Most current handguns have what are termed "three-dot" sights, meaning that the front sight has a dot of white paint (or a luminescent "night sight" embedded in it that appears as a round dot), and the rear sight has a white dot or night sight on each side of the notch. Lots of shooters find themselves confused: Do you put the white, front-sight dot in the center of the target? Or do you put the top of the front sight where you want to hit as described in the previous paragraph?

The correct answer is the second option. Putting the white front-sight dot in the middle of your target will obscure targets that are more than 10 or 15 yards out, and cause most of your shots to go high. Now, it goes without saying that most deadly confrontations occur at very close range, and in that case just plaster that front sight—white dot and all—in the center of the uncivilized fellow in question and turn loose. But for those of you who want to master your handgun and learn to get the most out of it, you'll need to learn fine sight alignment. William Tell sure couldn't have shot an apple off of his son's head with his crossbow by just plastering a white dot over the fruity vicinity.

When using adjustable rear sights, which a few models have or are available with as an option, adjusting your point of impact to perfection with any type of ammo you choose is possible. However, adjustable sights are less robust and more likely to snag clothing and whatnot than are fixed sights, so most defense-type handguns come with fixed sights. If you hit consistently left or right, it's usually possible to drift the rear sight a few thousandths left or right in its dovetail to compensate, but if you hit high or low, you need to either change bullet weights, trying various weights until one hits where you want it to; or change front sights.

Learn to shoot from "retention," where you hold the gun (in this case a plastic training gun) close to the body so that an attacker can't easily take it from you or push it away.

hree-dot sights can be confusing. Don't cover the enter of your target with them unless it's very, very lose—doing so is a good way to obscure the point ou're trying to hit.

Put the point you want to hit right on top of the front sight "flat." With your sights correctly zeroed, you'll punch the center out of a target at 15 yards or so.

I usually shoot half a dozen good defense loads of various weights through a new handgun, from a solid sandbag rest as described in the section on positions, and with any ort of luck one will both group accurately and hit where I want it to. That's what I then carry in the handgun, and I use similar-weight inexpensive FMJ (full metal jacket) loads or practice. Only in extreme cases do I purchase and install a different-height front sight, r send the gun to a gunsmith or back to the factory for a different sight.

For what it's worth, small variations are perfectly acceptable. Commonly, your point f impact—if off at all—will be slightly high at 25 yards, as in two or three inches. That's k. In fact, many action-pistol competitors prefer to have their bullets hit just slightly

Adjustable sights are bit less durable than fixed models, but they sure are easier to fine tune to hit where you want them to.

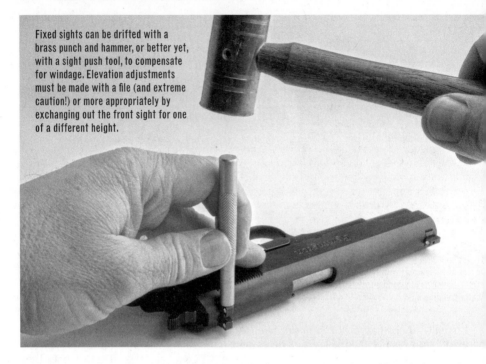

Fixed sights can be drifted with a brass punch and hammer, or better yet, with a sight push tool, to compensate for windage. Elevation adjustments must be made with a file (and extreme caution!) or more appropriately by exchanging out the front sight for one of a different height.

high, because that allows them to hold on the lower portion of steel knock-down plates which in turn allows them to see plates falling better—or not falling, as the case may be so they can re-shoot any they missed.

Sights that hit low are much less common, but are more of an issue than those that impact slightly high because—in order to place your shot where you want it—you've go to obscure your target. In this case, if I can't find a load that hits to point of impact, I'l change the front sight.

TRIGGER CONTROL

The final leg of the performance triad is the simplest, yet is also the most difficult to master. Why? Because it's the apex action that causes instant, painful recoil and intense levels of painful sound. Your body doesn't like that. Just as you'd wind your whole body up to jump a wide, deep creek, and then mentally shout "NOW!" and launch with every thing you've got, your inner mind wants to key up all your nerves and then suddenly and forcefully yank the trigger, anticipating the recoil and tensing—pushing into it—and in every way attempting to control the coming painful recoil and sound before it can hur you.

All that drama is absolutely death on accuracy.

Follow-through while shooting is more critical than in basketball, golf, or just abou any other sport. Really. You've got to discipline your mind to maintain the great positior and sight picture you've achieved, knowing that a tremor of nerves that only affects you hold by a few thousandths of an inch is more than enough to throw your shot wide, and you've got to squ-e-e-e-ze that trigger.

When you've got the time, slowly increase the pressure on the trigger, knowing that it will "break" within seconds but never allowing yourself to mentally shou "NOW!" and crush it. When the trigger breaks and the gun fires, it should surprise your reflexes. The detonation won't actually surprise you, of course, because you're the one commanding the finger that just slowly pressed the trigger, but it will sur prise your nerves and reflexes and the shot will be gone before they can tense and wrench the shot astray.

It's more difficult when you don't have time, as in when you're shooting rapid-fire in a match or desperately trying to put down a big hairy bad guy that's about to end your earthy sojourn. You don't have the luxury of a slow, controlled squeeze that will surprise your reflexes and allow you to get the shot off with perfect follow-through. Instead, you've got to mentally force yourself to hold that handgun steady and press through the trigger in fast, controlled pulls.

A correct grip, clenched until the blood almost drips, helps. When your muscles are that engaged, it's physically harder for them to release and jump in a different direction, as when anticipating recoil and pushing into it. A light-recoiling gun helps, too, because your body is more willing to hold steady under its light punishment than that of a heavier-recoiling gun. This is why so many people can shoot a 9mm exponentially faster than a .45 Auto. A truly proficient shooter can shoot a .45 darn near as fast as a 9mm, but most shooters can't.

The only way to master accurate rapid-fire shooting is extensive practice. Start with light-recoiling guns, return to the basics often to ensure a correct foundation, and practice. Then practice some more.

That said, quality practice is far more important than quantity. If you find yourself building a bad habit, don't press on through several more magazines of ammo, trying against all common sense to fix it when your muscles and mental focus are fatigued. Put your stubborn pride aside and fix it another day.

A small but related important rapid-fire skill is that of controlling the forward movement of the trigger after each shot. Forward movement is necessary in order to enable the trigger's sear to reset, but a quality trigger mechanism minimizes the amount of movement necessary, and good technique minimizes finger movement to just enough to reliably reset that quality trigger.

With correct position, sight alignment, and trigger control, handguns can be very effective, even when distances stretch a bit.

Good shooting when in a desperate hurry to stop something really bad from happening requires both steely nerves and a solid position and grip. In low light and at very close distances, sight alignment and trigger control take a back seat to recoil control, which is key to fast follow-up shots.

> *Skill built through dedicated practice will help you get the most out of your handgun.*

Dry-fire practice can help teach the mind and muscles the exact point the reset occurs with your preferred handgun. Good rapid-fire shooting begins slowly—teach your body the elements and put them together in slow motion, gradually increasing the shooting pace, never exceeding your skill level to the point where shooting becomes erratic. Eventually, you'll be able to rat-tat-tat-tat a target plate like a steel drum.

Remember the performance triad. If your shooting begins to come apart at the seams, run through your mental checklist and confirm the presence of each vital element and skill. Position. Make sure that your stance is solid, enabling you to hold your handgun steady and absorb recoil. Confirm that your grip is correct and firm, enabling control, precision, and speed. Sight alignment. Verify that you are achieving consistent alignment both within your sights and in how you place the sights on your target, and confirm that your sidearm is correctly sighted in. Trigger control. Master your jumpy nerves and discipline yourself into squeezing the trigger slowly when doing precision shooting and into following through like a bronze statue when shooting rapid fire. Never let the recoil control you; you control it. Return frequently to dry-fire practice to polish foundational skills and weed out blossoming bad habits.

With familiarity comes confidence. Pride and ego have no place around firearms, and never, ever win out against the unconscious confidence of long familiarity with a quality sidearm. An iota of talent mixed with the skill built through dedicated practice will help you get the most out of your handgun.

CHAPTER 12:

GET THE MOST OUT OF YOUR SHOTGUN

Shotguns are legendary as the ultimate close-range fight-stopper. From the highwaymen of yore, who stuffed whatever likely looking projectiles they could scrounge into the bell-shaped muzzles of their blunderbusses, to the cutoff double-barrel-carrying Wells Fargo stagecoach guards of the Old West, to the modern homeowner armed with a short-barreled pump gun with a heat shield and a toothy "persuader" compensator on its muzzle, folks have always trusted scatterguns when the going gets really dicey.

And why not? They are robust, simple to function, and forgiving when it comes to shot placement. Yet way too many folks take their shotgun skills for granted. There's more to getting the best out of your fighting fowling piece than just pointing it and pulling the trigger.

While shotguns are more forgiving than rifles or handguns, don't take your scattergunning skills for granted. Build your ability with correct technique.

Get on the balls of your feet and lean into that blunderbuss. Recoil from most 12-gauge shells is substantial enough to inhibit fast follow-up shots unless you're prepared for it.

THE PERFORMANCE TRIAD

As with a handgun and a rifle, there are three foundational skills pertinent to defensive shotgunning. Without all three, shot placement and effective firepower diminish, and recoil is much harder to control.

The three legs of this performance triad are position, sight alignment, and trigger control.

Position, in the case of shotgunning, covers stance, and grip with both the trigger hand and the support hand. Building a correct stance is vital to controlling the massive recoil generated by most shotguns and getting back on target quickly for follow-up shots.

Sight alignment is a pretty flexible term in shotgunning, since a shotgun is properly just pointed, as naturally as you'd point your finger. The exception is, of course, shotguns fitted with iron sights, which are useful for accurately shooting slugs.

Buckshot is far more applicable to personal defense purposes than slugs, and a sight-free barrel with a simple bead at the muzzle is most appropriate for shooting buckshot. However, since so many protection-type scatterguns have iron sights, and since there are conceivable uses for slugs in apocalyptic scenarios, we'll discuss both systems.

Trigger control is less of an issue with shotguns, which is perhaps a good part of why folks like them: most people can be lethal with a shotgun even without polished, hard-to-master skills like a disciplined trigger pull. But though squeezing like a benchrest competitive shooter isn't particularly useful while shooting a shotgun, there are still aspects of trigger control that are worth mastering.

Here's a breakdown of each skill set, as it applies to shotgun shooting.

POSITION (STANCE AND GRIP)

Shooting a shotgun is rarely a static activity. On the contrary, it's typically a moving, evolving attempt on an active target. So correct shotgun position is less about building a very stable stance for accuracy purposes than it is about building a stance that is both flexible—allowing the shooter to adapt to the target's movement—and at the same time is rock solid, enabling the shooter to offset the unbalancing effect of rigorous recoil and get off fast, effective follow-up shots.

Defensive shotshells typically kick significantly more than light loads intended for shooting clay targets. On top of that, defensive-type shotguns are shorter barreled and, unless you've hung a bunch of tactical garbage on it, lighter than sporting shotguns. Combined, the two elements add up to increased recoil. To achieve fast, effective follow-up shots, you've got to have a position and stance that allows you to soak up that recoil without getting pushed off balance by it.

The best shotgunning position will vary depending on the shooter's body type, strength, and other physical characteristics. A good place to start is with your feet shoulder width apart, the left foot (for right-handed shooters) a little ahead of the right foot. As you raise the shotgun to engage the target, lean into it, putting the bulk of your weight on the balls of your feet, and hunch your back and shoulders so that your shoulders are ahead of your hips, and your head is ahead of your shoulders. Roll your shoulders in and focus your energy and balance downrange.

Grip the shotgun firmly but not with a stranglehold. The trigger hand should not be sucked right up against the trigger guard (on classic type pistol grips), but rather should be located somewhat low on the curve of the grip to reduce the amount of torque in the shooting-hand wrist. The support hand should grip the forend with the index finger laid against it rather than wrapped around it, and that finger should point the same general direction as the barrel. You'd be surprised how much that helps achieve fast target acquisition.

From there, every shooter has to adapt and perfect the stance to what works best,

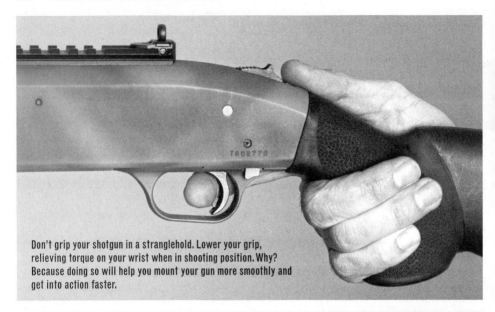

Don't grip your shotgun in a stranglehold. Lower your grip, relieving torque on your wrist when in shooting position. Why? Because doing so will help you mount your gun more smoothly and get into action faster.

working with it and finessing it through trial and error.

Once perfected, a single shot should barely rock the shooter. Even several shots in rapid succession shouldn't jar you out of position. If you find yourself rocked back on your heels (and in the beginning you will, rather often), your stance still needs work. With enough practice, you'll be able to turn loose a devastating stream of buckshot with shocking speed and effect.

SIGHT ALIGNMENT

If your shotgun is equipped with a classic bead front sight but no rear, the correct method of aiming is to just point the gun. In fact, good point shooters don't even need the bead—most can shoot just as well without one. The key is to build a consistent "mount."

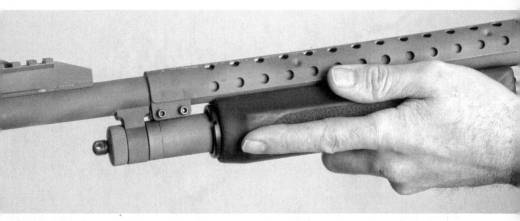

Grip the forend of your scattergun comfortably, with your index finger laying down it and pointing the same general direction as the muzzle. Most of the time you point a shotgun instead of aiming, and that pointed finger will help you get on target fast.

Practice mounting the gun—bringing it into shooting position, stock to the cheek first, shooting-eye looking down the barrel, then stock snug into the shoulder—until the movement is ingrained into your muscle memory and you do it the same way every time. Then forget about it and simply focus your attention on your target. All of it. Zone everything out and just let your muscle memory bring the gun into position and your subconscious mind point the gun.

It takes practice to achieve perfect focus clear through the shot. The tendency is to glance at the bead or barrel, consciously confirming your aim. Don't. Your subconscious mind is way ahead, and if you'll let it, it'll guide your shot perfectly every time.

> *No matter how rudimentary your skill level, your shotgun will do its best for you, which can't necessarily be said about a handgun or rifle.*

It is worth noting that you'll want to pattern your shotgun by firing it at a small spot on a large piece of paper 15 yards or so distant. Often a gun hits a little high or a little low, and you can either adjust your cheek weld so that you look down the barrel from a little higher or a little lower, thus finessing your point of impact to where you want it, or you can learn to compensate by holding a bit high or a bit low.

On the other hand, if your shotgun is fitted with iron sights, you'll need to learn to use them consistently. Most shotgun iron sights are "ghost ring" sights—wherein the rear is a small-diameter peep with a very large aperture. When looking through, the outline of the peep is there but fuzzes out, minimizing the amount that the sight obscures your target. In personal protection scenarios, that's a good thing.

The other somewhat common option is a typical rear barrel sight, with a flat top and a U-notch or square-bottomed notch. Typically, the matching front is a bead or sometimes a post.

Lining up the two exactly the same every time is key to consistency. In the case of a ghost ring rear, the eye will naturally center the front sight in the rear aperture. If your shotgun has a barrel sight, be sure to keep the front sight centered in the rear notch, side

Slugs aren't called for that often in the sphere of personal protection, but if you do need one, slow down and shoot your shotgun like a rifle, using the sights if present and sque-e-e-e-zing that trigger. I know—it kicks; grit your teeth if you have too.

to side, and the top of a flat-top post front sight (assuming that's what you have) even with the flat top of the rear sight.

If your front sight is a bead, float it in the rear sight using whatever sight picture you can repeat most consistently.

Point of impact with slugs should be exactly at the top of the front sight at about 25 yards. Typically, ghost-ring rear sights are adjustable for windage and elevation, allowing shooters to finesse their point of impact into perfection.

With buckshot, you want your sights pretty well centered in the pattern produced by the pellets.

TRIGGER CONTROL

Rarely will a good shotgun shooter ever actually squeeze a trigger. In most cases, there just isn't time. On moving targets, savvy shooters "slap" the trigger—lightly touching it off while maintaining lead and follow-through. It's difficult to do and still avoid anticipating the shot and tensing, pushing into the expected recoil and throwing off the shot before it ever has a chance, but with practice, it can be done.

When dumping a series of shots—whether at a target or into a deserving attacker— trigger control should mirror good rapid-fire handgun trigger technique more than anything else. Hold firm, follow through, and time your trigger press in rhythm with your recovery from recoil so that you neither send errant shots over the target nor waste time putting more lead into it.

Slug shooting is the only appropriate time to squeeze a shotgun trigger. Out to 50 or 60 yards, a properly fired slug can be placed with almost as much precision as a rifle bullet, if the shooter can achieve a steady position, a consistent sight picture, and squeeze the trigger. It's not easy, slugs hit like a miner's sledgehammer on both ends.

All three groups of the performance triad must be mastered to get the ultimate performance out of your scattergun, but the great beauty of a shotgun is that even if those skills are not completely mastered, even if they are rusty, undeveloped, or incomplete, your shotgun is still a pretty formidable personal protection tool. Practice, polish those skills, because a shotgun in the hands of a truly proficient shooter is a shockingly effective defense tool. But meanwhile, believe in your shotgun, because no matter how rudimentary your skill level, it will do its best for you, which can't necessarily be said about a handgun or rifle.

CHAPTER 13

GET THE MOST OUT OF YOUR RIFLE

Rifles are without doubt the most versatile firearms available. No other tool enables a shooter to effectively engage a target from zero distance to several hundred yards. And while rifles are not quite as easy to master as shotguns, they are much easier than handguns.

While this book isn't intended to teach advanced technique and turn readers into über-snipers capable of pulling off half-mile shots on uncivilized ruffians threatening home and country, there are certain basic steps to setting up a rifle, and skills vital to shooting one most effectively, that are worth discussing.

Rifles are very capable personal protection firearms, but to get the most out of yours—whatever you choose—you need to learn to shoot it fast and hard as well as slowly and precisely.

Within the confines of a home, even a compact rifle is far less maneuverable than a handgun, as demonstrated when attempting to peek—and if necessary shoot—around a corner in a direction opposite your natural shooting stance.

Rifles are akin to fine musical instruments: without a little tuning you'll never get the best out of them; yet with a little understanding and tweaking you can make them sing like a nightingale.

THE PERFORMANCE TRIAD

As with a handgun, good rifle shooting takes three skill sets—the performance triad. Without all three skill sets present and accounted for, accuracy goes awry.

The three are position, sight alignment, and trigger control.

The first is position, which, in the case of rifle shooting, primarily focuses on supported positions (kneeling, sitting, prone, and improvised) along with standing—typically known as "off-hand"—for fast action at smell-the-body-odor distances.

Why is position first? Because without a correct, stable position, neither of the other two legs of the performance triad can be accomplished.

At the risk of plagiarizing myself, I'm going to repeat a few sentences from the section on shooting handguns, because though the tool is different in size, the concept is identical:

Position is important because position is what lends stability to the firearm. No matter how perfect your sight alignment is, and how much trigger control you have, you can't consistently hit a target if your position doesn't prevent your gun from waving

n optic on a rifle offers ndeniable advantages, specially in low light or you've got weak vision. he 1.5-5X variable agnification scope n this AR-15 aids fast nooting at 20 yards or recise shooting at 400 ards, and the red-dot pping it makes for uper-fast head-up nooting at spitting istance.

around. Build a good, stable position, and you'll find that mastering sight alignment and trigger control is much easier.

Sight alignment is important because if your sights are (1) not regulated to place your bullet's impact on target and (2) you are personally incapable of lining them up exactly the same way for each and every shot, you'll never be able to predictably and consistently hit your target. Master sight alignment, pair it with a good position and excellent trigger control, and you will not only be able to hit your target predictably, you'll be able to place your shots exactly where you want them on that target.

Most rifles offer a potential sighting advantage not really applicable to handguns: optics. Almost any optical sight greatly simplifies consistent sighting by removing the need to line up a pair of sights on differing focal planes and then consistently plaster those sights on a target. With an optic you just put the dot or crosshair on the target and squeeze.

For defensive rifle shooting, use a position designed for soaking up recoil and getting you right back on target. Get your weight on the balls of your feet, crouch slightly, and lean forward, in effect turning your body into a spring. Extend your support arm, increasing your ability to point quickly and transition smoothly from target to target.

Trigger control is important because no matter how steady your position is, and no matter how perfectly and consistently you line up the sights, if you jerk the trigger and rattle the whole ensemble as the gun fires, hitting a target at all—let alone precisely—becomes purely a matter of luck. As with a handgun, trigger control is the third skill set on this list, but do not be fooled: it is also the apex. It's where all the others focus and come to fruition. Good trigger control is absolutely vital to good shooting.

Here's a breakdown of each skill set, as it applies to rifle shooting.

POSITION

There are two distinct position categories that are important to getting the best out of your rifle: unsupported (offhand) for speed and rapid fire (which is certainly the most useful in almost any self-defense situation in civilization's current scene); and supported,

For careful shots at long range, adopt an off-hand competitive-type stance. Slump, allowing skeletal support to take as much weight as possible, and keep your weight nicely balanced. Get your support-side elbow under the gun, breath deeply, and squeeze the trigger. Nope, this position won't be of much use in defending your life, but you should know how to shoot your rifle accurately anyway.

which is critical to precise shooting as distances stretch beyond 20 or 30 yards. Frankly, shooting another human at any distance past long loogey-hawking range is almost unjustifiable in our stable society; the precision-shooting ability you'll gain by polishing your position-shooting skills would come in handiest in an end-of-the-world-as-we-know-it scenario. But if you're going to shoot a rifle, you need to learn distance-shooting skills. Otherwise, you may as well just stick to a shotgun.

As a pleasant plus, those distance-shooting skills can be put to work putting venison on the family table.

First, let's discuss the offhand "fighting" rifle position. Most suitable to fast-and-furious action up close, a good fighting offhand position enables quick target engagement and good recoil control for rapid, on-target fire.

Not to be confused with the classic target-shooting offhand position, which strives for stability for slow, accurate shooting, the fighting offhand position discards stability in favor of mobility and resilience during recoil.

Start with your feet about shoulder width apart, with the left foot (for right-hand shooters) slightly ahead of the right, and the bulk of your weight on the balls of your feet. This helps avoid getting set back on your heels by recoil. Crouch just slightly, bending your knees enough to enable you to pivot right and left in an instant without getting off balance.

Grip the rifle's forend as far forward as is comfortable with the support hand (a technique proven by 3-gun competitive shooters to enhance fast target acquisition and transitions) and pull the stock firmly into the shoulder. Lean forward, hunching your shoulders like a gorilla and curving your body into a gentle forward curve, creating a

When available, use cover—both to reduce your vulnerability and to stabilize your rifle for more accurate shooting.

Learn to shoot from field positions, which are quick to get into and offer varying levels of support. Generally, the quickest positions are the least stable. Aside from offhand, unsupported, the kneeling position is the fastest. Squat on your heel and rest your support-side elbow on your knee to stabilize your rifle.

Sitting is one of the most useful field positions of all, quick and quite stable. Plant your rear firmly and dig your heels in at a slight offset to the target, and hook your elbows over your knees, getting as much skeletal support as possible.

The closer you get to the ground the more stable you become. Nothing beats prone with a bipod for accurate field shooting. Why do you need to know this? Because it's what rifles are really for.

human "spring" to counteract the effect of rapidly reoccurring recoil. Keep your strong-side elbow down if your rifle has a vertical trigger-hand grip; comfortably out if you have a traditional pistol grip.

With practice, you can whip a rifle up into position and on target with surprising speed. Better yet, once you turn loose on your target, you can unleash a hail of fire without getting rocked off balance—the weight-forward position and recoil-counteracting tension built into your position will counteract the effect of recoil. Sure, at first you may get pushed back on your heels now and then, but with practice you'll soak up the blunt hammering of your rifle and your sights will suck back onto target as if drawn by a magnet after each shot.

In the absence of a bipod or other rest, improvise. Create a rest out of your daypack, a stump, or anything else you can find.

A good prone position can be achieved quickly. From a walk you can drop to your knees and lunge forward, catching your fall with the butt of the rifle and then rolling into a prone shooting position.

Creating a stable supported position is a completely different game. The idea is to get as much physical contact with the ground or something solid (a table, doorjamb, windowsill, backpack, stump, or the like) as possible, then relax into it, removing as much muscle tension (and the resulting tremors) as possible.

A useful mantra is to get as close to the earth as possible. In the realm of positions, kneeling is more stable than standing; sitting more stable than kneeling, and prone more stable than any other position, especially with a bipod, backpack, or some other object to rest the rifle on.

I've seen shooters assume a "kneeling" position by just dropping to one knee, yet maintain an upright torso position without getting the support-hand elbow on the upright knee. What a waste. There's available skeletal support just screaming to be used (and skeletal support is always superior to muscular when striving for precision), yet being ignored—at the expense of accuracy. Kneel with the left foot forward (for right-handed shooters), get your butt down on the heel of the right foot, hunch forward, and get as much contact between your support-hand elbow and your knee as possible.

Then, relax. Maintain enough muscle tension to keep the rifle horizontal and in position, but don't fight to swing it right or left to get on target. Instead, let it find a natural point of aim, and then shift your feet to bring your sight right or left and on-target.

To build a good sitting position, drop on your behind with your body at an offset to the target, pivoted to the right for right-handed shooters and to the left for southpaws. Dig your heels into the ground about shoulder-width apart, knees upright, and lean forward at the waist, resting your elbows on your knees or even hooking them over your knees and gluing them to your shinbones if you're flexible enough. Relax, and allow your muzzle to settle to its natural point of aim, then shift your heels right or left to bring the rifle into alignment with the target.

(There are many variations of the sitting position, utilizing relaxed knees and crossed ankles with an extreme forward lean, and so on, but the position described above is relatively fast to assume and works for almost everybody, including less-flexible blokes like myself.)

Sitting is considerably more stable than kneeling. It takes just slightly longer to assume, but is absolutely worth it. I rarely use the kneeling position past 80 or 100 yards, but I'm quite confident shooting out to 200 or 250 from the sitting position.

Prone is another beast entirely. Without doubt, it is far and away the most stable, accurate field position. With practice, it can even be assumed with surprising speed. With a rest under the rifles forend, it's shockingly stable—a good rifleman with an accurate rifle can consistently hit small targets at obscene distances.

Though it may feel uncomfortable at first blush, with a little finessing a correct prone position allows the shooter to relax, making it very comfortable indeed once perfected. The basics aren't hard: get on your chest, plant your elbows firmly, and relax as much as possible while still keeping your rifle more or less horizontal. Scoot your butt to the right or left to adjust your point of aim right or left. Typically the torso will be somewhat offset from the rifle, angled to the left for right-handed shooters and vice versa.

Whatever rifle type you choose, learn to "stay in the scope" while functioning the rifle. It pays to be prepared for a fast follow-up shot.

> *Rifles shudder as a bullet travels down the barrel, and if rested on a hard object will bounce a little in the micro-seconds before the projectile exits the muzzle.*

To polish the position, try to get the support-hand elbow directly under the rifle, enhancing vertical support. Pull the left knee (for right-handers) up, easing tension on the lower back and lifting the abdomen slightly away from the ground, minimizing the influence of your heartbeat (which actually pulses more noticeably in the abdomen than the chest). Relax as much as possible, shifting your butt left and right to adjust horizontal point of aim and scooching it slightly forward or rearward to lower or raise point of aim.

Finally, if possible, get some sort of support under the rifle's forend. Bolting a folding bipod to the forend is a good option if you don't mind the bulk and weight, but more folks prefer to throw a light backpack down and rest over it, or find a natural object such as a rock or stump. Importantly, do not allow the rifle to rest directly on any hard object, as vibrations as the rifle fires will cause it to shoot high. Rifles shudder as a bullet travels down the barrel, and if rested on a hard object will bounce a little in the micro-seconds before the projectile exits the muzzle. Sandbags, backpacks, or even a glove or hat dropped over a rock eliminates the effect.

If precision is important to the success of a shot, always try to use the prone position—or some improvised variation on it utilizing a relaxed lean on a ditch bank, truck hood, windowsill or whatnot—with a steady rest under the forend. Unless there just isn't time, or the local architecture prevents it (think thigh-high grass that you can't see or shoot through), get prone.

Here's a process used to get into a prone position rapidly. Let's assume that you're strolling along a mountain ridge in search of winter meat and spot a good buck a couple of hundred yards distant, or that you're patrolling along the perimeter of your property six months after The Big Meltdown and spot a gang of thugs strangling Uncle Waldo 400 yards away. Speed and precision are both called for.

Step one: Without stalling your forward movement, drop to your knees. Step two: As your momentum causes you to fall forward from the knees, plant the butt of your rifle in the ground, slowing your decent (you'll want a two-hand grip on the rifle). Step three: Drop your left elbow to the earth, roll the butt of the rifle into your shoulder pocket, and settle your right elbow to the ground as your sights come onto your target.

You've got to be willing to take a few bruises learning to fall into the prone position smoothly, but it is well worth it.

If your chosen firearm is a bolt action (as it is likely to be if you are into precision shooting), it's also vital to learn to cycle the action quickly and smoothly without lifting your cheek from the stock or your eye from the optic or sights. Many folks—even most folks—lower the stock from their shoulder, lift their head, and cycle the bolt. What a waste of time and movement.

SIGHT ALIGNMENT

While you can point-shoot a villain with a shotgun, and even with a handgun when up close and personal, good sights are the tool that harnesses a rifle's distance potential. Sure, at across-the-couch distances a rifle can be point-fired effectively as well, but that really misses the point of a rifle. Learn to sight consistently, couple that skill with a good

Consistent sight alignment is critical to accurate shooting. With the "ghost-ring" type sights on most of today's fighting firearms it's easy—your eye will naturally center the front sight in the rear aperture or "peep" sight. Keeping the two aligned, put your target at the tip of the front sight and squeeze...

position and polished trigger control, and you'll add the ability to place shots with shocking precision at several hundred yards to your repertoire of personal protection tools.

These days, most of the more sophisticated rifles end up with an optic, which greatly simplifies consistent sighting. But many classic warhorses such as the legendary AK-47 are problematic for mounting an optic, and perform just fine without one at the distances for which they are intended. So we'll start by discussing iron-sight skills and then move on to using optics.

Post and notch sights such as these on an old Mauser military rifle are harder to master. Keep the front sight centered in the rear notch, and the top of the front sight level with the top of the rear.

No matter how accurate your rifle is, you won't get the best out of it if it's not properly sighted in. Whether using iron sights or an optic, adjust your sights until you hit perfect center at whatever distance you choose to "zero" at.

IRON SIGHTS

Rifle iron sights come in many types and variations. Most fighting experts agree that the best of the lot are those utilizing a large rear aperture—typically termed a "ghost ring" because as you look through it the outline partially hazes out, leaving an excellent field of view around it—coupled with a post-type front sight. Such apertures—also known as peep sights—help achieve consistency. Why? Because the eye naturally finds center in the rear aperture, and just as naturally brings the tip of the front sight to the center of the view through the aperture.

Most (but not all) military-type rifles designed since around WWII have aperture rear sights and a good, clean post front. However, AK-47s, SKSs, and most European bolt-actions (with the exception of several British variants) have what is termed an "open" rear sight with a flat-topped "U" notch, "V" notch, or square notch that marries with a post-type or pyramid-type front sight. So do the earlier Springfield 1903 rifles, as well as almost all hunting rifles.

To get the best out of both types of sights (aperture and open), the front sight must be aligned perfectly within the rear peep or notch every time. As you look through them, with the front blade nestled in the rear, ensure that you see equal space on each side of the front sight. With an open, notch-type rear, ensure that the front sight's top—whether flat or pointed—is perfectly level with the top of the flats to each side of a rear notch. With a peep, ensure that the front sight's top is perfectly centered in the rear aperture.

Maintaining that alignment, put the front sight on your target, squeeze the trigger, and—assuming your sights are correctly adjusted to compensate for trajectory—the rifle will do the rest.

Speaking of trajectory, as a bullet flies downrange it has an arced path, and you must adjust your sights (generally the rear) to compensate as distances stretch. For instance, if your .223 is sighted to impact dead on at 200 yards, the bullet's drop—trajectory—will

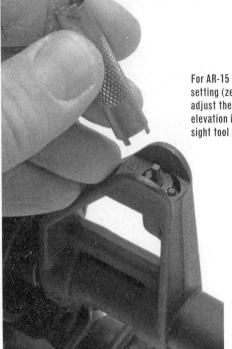

For AR-15 rifles, set your rear sight on the desired setting (zero, a specific yardage, or whatnot) and then adjust the height of your front sight post until impact elevation is perfect at your chosen distance. A simple AR sight tool makes screwing it up or down much easier.

Rear sights on common sporting rifles can be adjusted by loosening a screw and sliding the sight up, down, or right and left. Easy, but not very precise. Trial and error will get you there eventually.

cause it to impact low at 300 yards, and much lower at 400. With a good sight and a little understanding of how much your particular load drops (a function of projectile aerodynamics, weight, and velocity) at various distances, trajectory is easily compensated for.

Now, very importantly, no matter how consistent your sight alignment is, unless your sights are properly adjusted to place your bullet at the point of aim, you won't hit your target in the center. The distance at which a rifle's sights are set to exact point of impact is commonly referred to as the "zero." As in, "My rifle is zeroed at 200 yards."

Zeroing is accomplished by moving the sights up or down to compensate for vertical variation and right or left for horizontal variation.

With common high-performance rifle cartridges that push a bullet in excess of about 2,500 fps (feet per second), I prefer to sight my rifle to impact dead on at 200 yards. My bullet's path will be around a couple of inches high at 100 yards, and five to eight inches low at 300. It's a versatile zero that allows quite precise shooting from spitting distance out to three times the length of a football field.

With a slower cartridge, such as a 7.62x39mm (AK-47, SKS) or .30-30 Winchester (a typical lever-action cartridge), sight in at 100 yards, or perhaps 150. Due to the limited velocity (2,000 to 2,500 fps) and reduced aerodynamics of the projectiles such cartridges shoot, the outside edge of your really effective range is about 200 or 250 yards. A close zero prevents having your bullets path arch too high above your line of sight.

Any carbine chambered for a pistol caliber (.38 Special, .357 Magnum, .44 Magnum) should be sighted in at no more than 100 yards. The velocity offered is usually in the 1,000 to 1,600 fps range, and the bullets are the antithesis of aerodynamic. Past about 100 yards, the resulting dramatic curve in trajectory causes bullets to drop way below line of sight. While I've shot at targets (mostly ineffectively) in excess of 500 yards away with such rifles, they aren't particularly effective past about 150 yards or perhaps 200 in the hands of a very accomplished rifleman.

When you settle in to zero your rifle at your intended range, get as steady as possible, ideally over a pair of sandbags placed under the forend and the buttstock of your rifle, and fire a careful three-shot group before moving anything. Average the point of impact of the three bullet holes, adjust the sights accordingly, and then fire another three-shot group to confirm the correction. Finesse further as necessary.

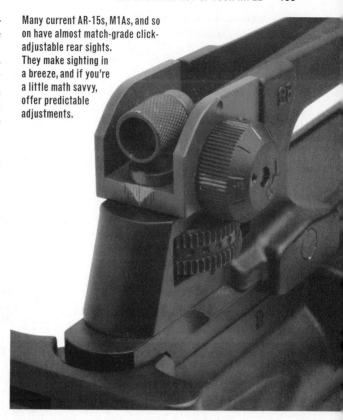

Many current AR-15s, M1As, and so on have almost match-grade click-adjustable rear sights. They make sighting in a breeze, and if you're a little math savvy, offer predictable adjustments.

Which direction to move the sight to compensate is often confusing. Here is a set of guidelines:

If moving the front sight:
- Adjust sight up to bring point of impact down
- Adjust sight down to bring point of impact up
- Adjust sight left to bring point of impact right
- Adjust sight right to bring point of impact left

If moving the rear sight:
- Adjust sight up to bring point of impact up
- Adjust sight down to bring point of impact down
- Adjust sight right to bring point of impact right
- Adjust sight left to bring point of impact left

Most military-type rear sights are marked with a scale of one sort or another indicating settings for various ranges, and the front sights are often adjustable, allowing the shooter to set the rear at the 100-yard mark (or 200 or whatever you prefer) and leave it there, screwing the front sight up or down until the rifle is zeroed. It goes without saying that this needs to be done at the correct distance.

The more sophisticated rear sights (such as those on M1As, M1 Garands, and most AR-15s) offer click-adjustable adjustments for elevation and windage. Once your front sight is adjusted to place your shots on target at your zero range, the click-adjustable sight becomes a valuable tool, enabling good shooters to make precise shots at very impressive distances.

■ OPTICAL SIGHTS

Optics simplify the sighting process significantly, and can make a tremendous difference for those with weak or aging vision. How? By taking the multi-depth focusing requirement out of the equation. Good optics put the sighting reticle or dot on the same plane as the target. Additionally, many optics magnify the target, enhancing precision dramatically.

(It's worth noting that anybody interested in scraping bad guys off the front porch with a firearm should become proficient with iron rifle sights before transitioning to an optic; it's another a skill that could save your life.)

Right up front, I'm going to steer you away from the most common, tragic mistake that plagues new optic buyers. If you only take one thing away from this section, let this be it: Buy the most expensive optic you can possibly afford. It boggles my mind that people think they can pay $60 for set of glass lenses, allegedly ground to perfect shape and coated in refraction- and reflection-reducing agents, mounted in perfect alignment in precision elevation and windage adjustment gears, and the whole of it slapped into a multidimensional aluminum tube and fog, shock, and waterproofed, and actually expect it to work. It's presumptuous to even hope that any optic for less than about $200 will serve ably and reliably, and the good stuff starts at about twice that and ranges up into the thousands of dollars.

For self-defense purposes, optics fall into two very broad categories: magnified and non-magnified. Non-magnified optics commonly offer a broad field of view, which is good when you're trying to see into every dark corner of the cottage at once, and assist fast target acquisition, another worthy attribute. Magnified optics, on the other hand, offer very precise shot placement by—surprise!—magnifying the target.

Simply put, if your rifle is primarily intended for use inside the home and for shooting inside 150 yards or so, go with a non-magnified optic or—my preference—a variable-power scope that runs from 1X to 4X magnification or 1.5X to 5X. Keep the magnification ring turned down to the lowest power for defense purposes, crank it up for longer shots.

Red dot sights don't offer the precision of a magnified optic, but they're faster and work great for folks who struggle to resolve iron sights.

When precision is important, build a stable position, sight carefully, and sque-e-e-eze that trigger.

"Tactical" scopes enable tremendous precision at extreme distances, but in reality can limit you in self-defense scenarios—too much magnification makes it very hard to find close-and-personal targets.

If your rifle is a precision job intended for use at long range, go with a magnified optic. Most magnified scopes today offer variable power, allowing you to choose something with plenty of high end that you can still dial down to 3X or 4X for closer work.

Reticles—the crosshair, dot, or other aiming device suspended inside the optic—are typically either etched into the glass or are electronic, sometimes both. Given my druthers, I'll always opt for etched reticles, because they work with or without batteries, but there are some fantastic electronic optics out there today, namely those by Aimpoint, Eotech, and their ilk.

> *Scopes don't sit right on the barrel like iron sights do, and often your point of impact will be way off.*

Once a scope is correctly leveled, proper eye relief is established, and the whole ensemble is bolted into place in a set of premium scope rings, sighting it in is usually much easier than sighting in iron sights, though the process is much the same.

There is one additional step, though. You've got to get your rifle impacting on paper at close range (25 yards or so) before stretching out to your final desired zero distance. Scopes don't sit right on the barrel like iron sights do, and often your point of impact will be way off—we're talking feet here—even up close.

Bore sighting can expedite the process, but in the end nothing replaces putting shots on paper. Staple up a big sheet of paper, or use a large piece of cardboard as a backer, so you can pinpoint shots that miss the actual target. Fire three shots, and adjust the elevation and windage turrets until your point of impact is an inch or two low at 25 yards (remember that the scope sits above the bore, putting your line of sight high at close range).

Most scope turrets move point of impact about 0.25 inch at 100 yards, or ¼ MOA, which is much the same for practical purposes. Some offer 0.5-inch 100-yard adjustments; others, commonly of European or military influence, move point of impact 0.1 Mil; which is about 10 millimeters or about 0.36 inch at 100 yards, per click.

When making adjustments at 25 yards, it is necessary to multiply the amount of clicks necessary to make a one-inch adjustment by four—the target is four times closer than

Most optics come with click-adjustable windage and elevation turrets. Each click will move point of impact a specified distance, such as 0.25 inch at 100 yards, or 0.25 MOA, or 1-tenth miliradian—terms you'll familiarize yourself with if you get into long-range recreational shooting, but pretty useless info on the personal protection scene.

100 yards. Conversely, at 200 yards you reduce the number of clicks by half—the target is twice as far away. And so on.

Once you move to your final zero distance, take your time. Shoot careful three-shot groups, make appropriate adjustments, and let your rifle cool between groups. You don't want a hot barrel causing groups to open up, point of impact to wander, and your frustration to cause a meltdown every bit as hot as the rifle barrel inspiring it.

The technical aspect of the myriad variations of high-performance optics would fill a good-sized book, let alone how-to information, so I'll leave the in-depth research to you, the World Wide Web, and your local gunshop.

Just remember: Buy the most expensive optic you can possibly afford.

TRIGGER CONTROL

For precision shooting—which is what rifles are all about—trigger control is critical. Time to plagiarize myself again and refer to the trigger control section in Chapter 11 on handgun shooting:

This final leg of the performance triad is the simplest, yet is also the most difficult to master. Why? Because it's the apex action that causes instant, painful recoil and intense levels of painful sound. Your body doesn't like that. Just as you'd wind your whole body up to jump a wide, deep creek, and then mentally shout "NOW!" and launch with everything you've got, your inner mind wants to key up all your nerves and then suddenly and forcefully yank the trigger, anticipating the recoil and tensing—pushing into it—and in every way attempting to control the coming painful recoil and sound before it can hurt you.

All that drama is absolutely death on accuracy.

Follow-through while shooting is more critical than in basketball, golf, or just about any other sport. Really. You've got to discipline your mind to maintain the great position and sight picture you've achieved, knowing that a tremor of nerves that only affects your hold by a few thousandths of an inch is more than enough to throw your shot wide, and squ-e-e-e-ze that trigger.

When precision is important, take a couple of deep breaths to slow your heartbeat, and hold that breath partway out or all the way out. Slowly increase the pressure on the trigger, knowing that it will "break" within seconds but never allowing yourself to mentally shout "NOW!" and crush it. When the trigger breaks and the gun fires, it should surprise your reflexes. The detonation won't actually surprise you, of course, because

Many rifle skills aren't particularly useful in today's fairly tame society where you'd better be very, very sure your life is in real danger before defending yourself. However, if you believe in being prepared for the worst—in whatever form a monumental disaster might take—a rifle would be your single most effective tool, and skill with it would be invaluable.

you're the one commanding the finger that just slowly pressed the trigger, but it will surprise your nerves and reflexes and the shot will be gone before they can tense and wrench the shot astray.

It's more difficult when you don't have time, as in when you're shooting rapid-fire in a 3-gun match or desperately trying to put down a big hairy bad guy that's about to end your earthy sojourn. You don't have the luxury of a slow, controlled squeeze that will surprise your reflexes and allow you to get the shot off with perfect follow-through. Instead, you've got to mentally force yourself to hold your sights steady on the target and press through the trigger in fast, controlled pulls. A practiced shooter can dump an astonishing amount of accurate close-range fire.

Your rifle—assuming you made a good choice when purchasing it, and put in the setup and practice time necessary to get the best out of it—is a tool that enables you to handle any life-threatening adversary from spitting distance to several hundred yards. It's more powerful than a handgun, and more accurate than either a handgun or shotgun. It's precise. Personally, being something of a rural kind of guy, if forced to choose just one type of firearm for personal protection, I'll take a rifle every time. Now, if I lived in downtown New York City, I'd likely choose a handgun. But I don't.

While such discussion is a bit far-fetched most of the time, there's one life-threatening scene wherein a rifle beats the other options all hollow: that of an end-of-civilization scenario. Whether prompted by nationwide financial collapse, disastrous storms, hostile government takeover, or something simple like the zombie apocalypse, you'd be best armed to survive a world of riots, enemy occupiers, and cannibalism with a rifle. Though dangerous encounters in such a time could often be close, the ability to fend off threats as far away as possible would be critically important.

Getting the most out of your rifle demands dedication, but the rewards are exponential—put in a little time, gain a lot of performance. If you find that you are spinning your wheels, or that your accuracy is degrading, refer back to the performance triad and rebuild the foundation of your rifle shooting skill set. And then polish that foundation with a mansion of fine-tuned skills. Shoot 3-gun matches to hone rapid-fire action-shooting skills. Shoot High-Power matches to enhance your precision shooting and wind-reading abilities. And if you possibly can, hunt. There's no substitute for time spent in the field using your rifle with real intent, providing food and thus protecting your family from the ravages of winter. No class, however good, can gain you the same insights and abilities.

CHAPTER 14:

CARE AND MAINTENANCE

A firearm, like even the very best of trusted friends, will eventually go south on you without a little care and maintenance. And according to Murphy's Law, it will probably do so at the worst possible moment, leaving you without a sidearm to fight off the big hairy bad guy.

Assuming that your firearm is good quality, it doesn't take much to keep it running perfectly, except perhaps in the case of AR-15-type rifles. Many combat-proven guns can take an astonishing amount of battlefield abuse and keep on functioning perfectly, particularly AK-47s, M14s (or their civilian counterpart, the M1A), most 1911s, Glocks, and so on.

There are two different aspects of a firearm that must be kept relatively clean for optimum performance: the action and the bore (inside of the barrel).

Clean, AR-15-type rifles are very reliable. Cut off Murphy at his roots and rigorously maintain the tools on which your life may depend.

CLEANING THE ACTION

Semiautomatic firearms require the most cleaning, especially in the action portion. If you've never cleaned yours, dig up a manufacturer's manual and learn to field strip and reassemble it first.

Once you've got it field stripped, wipe all powder fouling, sand, lint, and other crud off of all the various parts with a solvent-soaked rag. Carbon buildup from powder can be seemingly impossible to remove, especially on the bolt of AR-15 rifles, but persist with solvent, brushes, and if appropriate, a fouling scraper until it's gone. On rifles, pay particular attention to the face of the bolt, the bolt locking lugs, and the extractor.

Clean inside the action, scrubbing all surfaces and wiping them clean, especially contact surfaces. Though it can be a struggle, get inside the locking lug recesses of rifles as best you can.

Due to their operating systems, AR-15s tend to build up a lot of carbon fouling inside the guts of the action. Don't hesitate to get aggressive—with proper tools—and clean it off. Here, a fouling scraper flakes off a layer built up on the tail of an AR bolt.

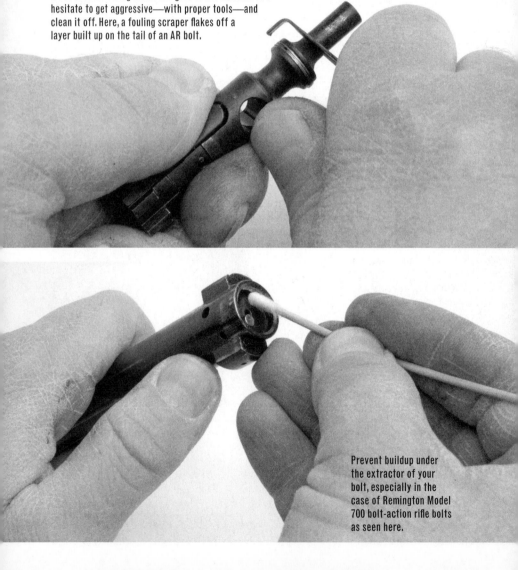

Prevent buildup under the extractor of your bolt, especially in the case of Remington Model 700 bolt-action rifle bolts as seen here.

If you're in the field and just don't have the time, or maybe the tools, to correctly clean your AR-15, a generous dash of CLP (Cleaner Lubricant Preservative) will help keep it running reliably even when dirty.

Good lubricants come in many forms. Use those specified for firearms—you don't want your action slathered with a lube that will gel after a few months and gum up the works.

In typical climates with plenty of humidity and low dust, I tend to coat all metal surfaces inside and out with a film of oil, applying lubricant fairly generously on contact surfaces. Be sure to use a proper gun lubricant, so that it doesn't gel or coagulate over time and gum up your gun. Many lesser oils lose their lubricity over time and can create a real headache when they congeal inside moving parts.

There are two types of climate and one environmental condition that require special treatment. Very corrosive climates (like seaside areas with high humidity and salt content) demand more aggressive preventive care—in essence more oil, more frequently. Very dry climates (with the usual copious amounts of dust and sand) suggest less oil, because oil attracts and traps grit, sand, and dust, which crud can slow down or even stop

In very arid climates, dust is your enemy and excessive oil attracts dust. Use minimal lube, applied to key points that keep your gun running. In such climates, corrosion usually isn't a problem.

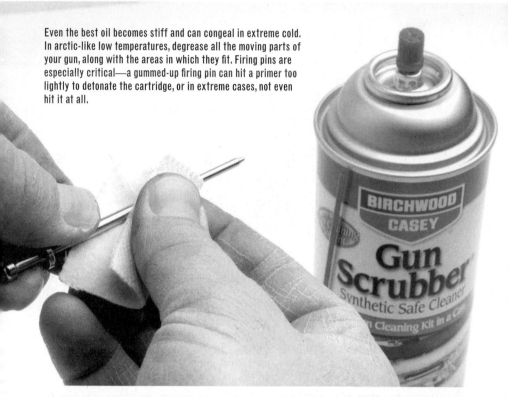

Even the best oil becomes stiff and can congeal in extreme cold. In arctic-like low temperatures, degrease all the moving parts of your gun, along with the areas in which they fit. Firing pins are especially critical—a gummed-up firing pin can hit a primer too lightly to detonate the cartridge, or in extreme cases, not even hit it at all.

moving parts. In such arid climates I tend to oil very lightly, and only on moving parts and contact/friction areas. Usually, rust and corrosion doesn't occur much in such areas.

Finally, in extremely cold temperatures (the environmental condition) you may not want to have oil in your gun at all. We're talking way below freezing here, where it's so frigid that even the best of oils will congeal from the cold and can cause your gun to malfunction. A classic example is when hunting bears far north of the arctic circle, where a little oil on the firing pin of your usually reliable bolt-action can cause the firing pin to be so sluggish that it won't detonate a primer and fire the cartridge in your chamber—rather a disconcerting occurrence when within spitting distance of an aggravated bear.

Though I use dedicated solvents, copper solvents, and lubricants frequently, if you really want to keep it simple just get a high-end CLP (cleaner, lubricant, preservative) and use it for everything. Developed for military use, it does a good job of breaking down powder fowling, lubing moving parts and contact surfaces, and protecting your gun from corrosion.

One thing it doesn't do well is remove copper fouling (residue from the copper-jacketed bullet) from the rifling of your barrel, which leads us to cleaning barrels.

CLEANING THE BARREL

Handgun barrels are pretty easy, unless they've gotten "leaded" up, meaning lead from a cast or swedged-lead bullet more or less got soldered into the rifling. Leading can be difficult to remove—more on that toward the end of this chapter. For common cleaning, just scrub your handgun barrels with a mild solvent and a bronze or nylon-bristle brush, wipe them out with cotton patches on a correctly-fitting jag, then oil to prevent corrosion.

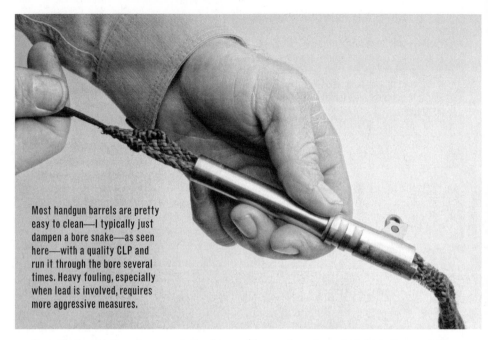

Most handgun barrels are pretty easy to clean—I typically just dampen a bore snake—as seen here—with a quality CLP and run it through the bore several times. Heavy fouling, especially when lead is involved, requires more aggressive measures.

For rifle barrel cleaning, scrub the bore with a series of good stout cotton patches on a jag of correct size, pushed by a coated, non-abrasive, non-jointed rod of high quality. Push the patches through from the breach if possible, allowing them to fall off after exiting the muzzle. There's no need to pull dissolved fouling gunk and grit back into your rifling.

Always clean barrels from the rear if you can, so you don't push fouling and gunk into the chamber and locking lug recesses and the action. Use a one-piece cleaning rod—jointed rods flex at the joints and can abrade rifling.

If you can't clean a rifle barrel from the rear with a rod, use a pull-through flexible rod and clean it from the rear anyway. For deep cleaning you many need to use a rod from the muzzle, but be sure to protect the crown of your barrel with a bore guide.

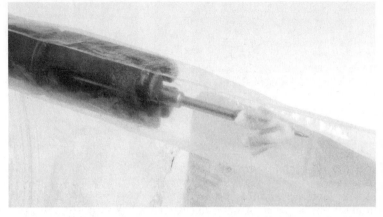

You can purchase patch-catching devices, but a zip-lock bag over the muzzle works just as well. When it's full of dirty, solvent-soaked patches, just seal it up and dispose of it.

(Tip: Use a sturdy zip-lock bag over the muzzle of your rifle to catch dripping solvent and dirty patches. Insert a couple of inches of barrel and snug the zip up around it. When you're done cleaning, just slide off the baggie, zip it shut, and your mess is contained.)

Lever-action rifles, semiautos, and pump-actions usually must be either cleaned from the muzzle with a rod (use a bore guide to protect the crown from wear), or cleaned from the breach with a pull-through setup such as those from Otis or a Hoppe's Bore Snake. Unless you're dealing with serious copper fouling, I prefer the pull-through rig because it doesn't deposit gunk into the action.

Follow the wet patches with several passes of a bronze bristle brush of correct size (I'm superstitious and usually make the same amount of passes with the brush as the number of shots I've fired through that barrel since the last cleaning, unless the round count is over 20—in that case, I stop there). Finally, follow the scrubbing with a series of wet and dry patches.

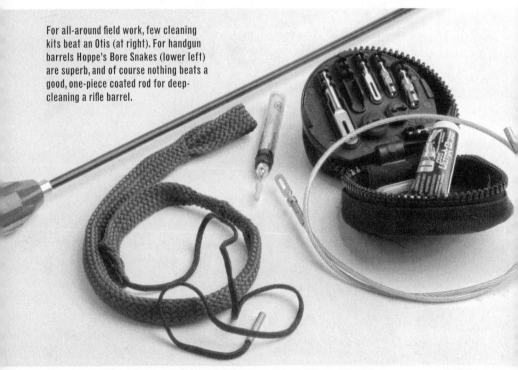

For all-around field work, few cleaning kits beat an Otis (at right). For handgun barrels Hoppe's Bore Snakes (lower left) are superb, and of course nothing beats a good, one-piece coated rod for deep-cleaning a rifle barrel.

Rare are the factory production barrels that will come clean in a single session, though top-notch match-grade custom barrels typically will do so. Usually I have to leave a production factory barrel to soak with solvent in it, and come back one or more times and repeat the wet/dry patch sequence.

Many shooters damage the insides of their barrels by cleaning with a multi-piece rod of several sections that screw together. The joints flex, creating points that abrade the rifling. A good one-piece rod eliminates that. Sure, it's hard to pack around, but so what. A damaged barrel does you no good. For a field cleaning kit, get a flexible pull-through system.

Another thing to avoid is rods of steel (they're harder on barrels than coated rods) and rods of brass or aluminum, which don't directly cause wear on your rifling but can host imbedded grit that does.

Copper fouling tends to build more heavily in some barrels than in others,

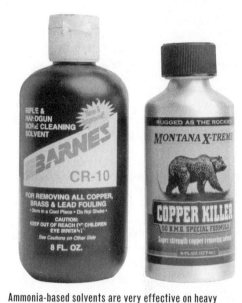

Ammonia-based solvents are very effective on heavy copper fouling. But be cautious with their use and make sure and flush your bore aggressively afterward—even traces left in your bore for periods of more than 10 to 20 minutes can etch your rifling.

particularly barrels with rough internal surfaces, and can be a bear to remove. It can and usually does degrade accuracy, so you'll need to get it out every so often.

Most shooters use ammonia-based solvents to remove copper. It dissolves copper particularly well, but unfortunately it also dissolves pretty much all metal and, left unattended in your barrel, can etch the internal surfaces horribly and destroy your barrel. If you use an ammonia-based solvent, use it with great caution.

Modern solvents are effective on both powder fouling and copper fouling, and are harmless to barrel steels and most—but not all—stock finishes. Sharp Shoot-R's Wipe-Out bore cleaner is one of the best.

A four-time Swedish Olympic team shooter once told me that nothing ruins more guns than ammonia solvents. He never uses it. When I asked him how to neutralize ammonia if you do need to use it, the reply was to flush your barrel with copious amounts of warm water after cleaning, and flush again every day for the next three days. According to him, the real issue is that most shooters never get all the ammonia solvent out of their barrels, leaving traces in the micro-fractures and pores in the steel. The result? Those micro-fractures get eaten into "small canyons" in the surfaces of the steel. That can't be good.

Shortly after that discussion, I was turned on to a foaming solvent called Wipe Out and its standard-type solvent sibling, Patch Out. I don't know what kind of wizardry goes into mixing it, but it's death on copper and allegedly completely harmless to steel and most stock finishes (though I have accidentally taken the oil finish off a workbench or two and damaged the old-school varnish-based paint on an early Kevlar stock with it). I now use copious quantities of both Patch Out and Wipe Out.

If your gun is one of the rare breed that just doesn't tend to accumulate copper in the barrel, stick with a mild fouling solvent such as Hoppe's 9. It will both clean your barrel and preserve it from corrosion.

After cleaning, dry the bore well with a series of clean, dry patches, and then apply CLP on a final clean patch. I figure that, even if I didn't get the bore spotlessly clean, the CLP will prevent corrosion and keep working on any remaining traces of fouling, softening it up and neutralizing it.

Back to cleaning "leading" out of a barrel—whether rifle or handgun: There are special lead-removing products that allegedly work, and you might have to try them. I've even—in desperation—used mesh copper patches to scrub lead out of barrels. It didn't work too well.

There are detractors of the practice, but I've had the best luck removing lead by just shooting a bunch of jacketed bullets through the barrel. It's said that doing so can cause pressure spikes in high-power rifle cartridges, and perhaps it's so. Frankly, I've never leaded up such a barrel, and can't say one way or the other. For handguns and pistol-caliber carbines, it works. Just be smart enough not to go back to the load that leaded your barrel.

While the cleaning methods described here work well for me, this is anything but a comprehensive, all-inclusive guide to firearm cleaning. There are many other useful methods, tools, and solvents.

MOVING PARTS

No chapter on firearm maintenance would be complete without discussing the potential for wear on moving parts and replacing broken parts. Here's my take on the topic: the best way to maintain the moving parts of your gun is to (1) purchase quality to start with and (2) keep it properly lubed. Yes, occasionally the parts on any gun can break, but for the most part high-quality firearms have a round-count life that far exceeds what the typical gun owner will put through them.

I am something of a pseudo gunsmith, and I work on a lot of guns, but almost all of that work is modifying or customizing—rarely do I replace worn or broken parts. Usually, if someone brings me a gun to "fix," all I have to do is a good deep clean and oil and, voila!, it runs like a top.

Is it worth keeping a selection of spare parts on hand? If you're a prepper, yes. If you tend to lose parts while fieldstripping and cleaning, yes. Otherwise, I wouldn't bother.

Keep it clean, keep it lubed, and keep it stored away from lint, dust, and grime. Take care of your gun, and when the chips are down, it will take care of you.

CHAPTER 15:

CUSTOMIZING

For foundational personal protection uses, quality firearms don't need customizing. They've been designed for hard use under degraded conditions, and rigorously tested to prove that they posses reliability, acceptable accuracy, and ergonomics that work well for most shooters.

That said, most of us like to personalize our possessions, and as gun owners become accomplished shooters, they begin to find attributes and nuances about their firearms that they do and don't appreciate. Grip shape and texture, trigger pull, type of sights, type of rifle stock and forend, and so forth can have an influence on how well and how comfortably you shoot a particular gun.

So... if you know what works best for you and have the handyman savvy to do the work, or the financial wherewithal to hire a good gunsmith to do it for you, why not customize your guns to be exactly the way you like them?

The above postulation comes with one very critical caveat: Never, ever make a modification that could potentially compromise the reliability of your firearm. The unfortunate truth is that many modifications have the potential to do so. In particular, the tolerances of match-grade parts can improve accuracy, but degrade reliability under dirty conditions; and often gun parts that improve some nuance—of trigger pull, for example—haven't been tested nearly as rigorously as the factory parts. Be cautious in how you "improve" your

Serious shooters like to swap out bits and pieces to make their favorite tools more to their liking. Just don't do anything that could compromise reliability.

gun—that improvement may come back to bite you if a cartridge fails to chamber, deto-nate, or extract, or if your trigger fails to cause your hand-cannon to go bang when you desperately need to scrape the big angry man with the axe off of the hood of your Volvo.

What sort of modifications are the most useful? That depends on personal taste, but for the most part user-possible modifications are limited to grip, trigger, and sight modifica-tions on handguns, and stock, fore-end, trigger, and sight mods on rifles such as AR-15s.

GRIPS

While quite a few fans of polymer guns modify their grip by stippling the polymer with a soldering iron or wood-burning tool, making the texture much more aggressive, I per-sonally don't think it's necessary. If you like it, and if it helps you shoot when conditions are less than optimal, go for it. The only reason I don't buy into the practice is that I don't want other guns of similar model to feel slippery or awkward in my hands after becoming accustomed to the modified one.

Taking the polymer-grip mod a bit further, some folks will remove material from key areas to make their grip fit their hand more perfectly. Removing material just under the trigger guard and at the top rear of the grip in particular allow a shooter to achieve a higher grip, making for better recoil control, but you've got to be really savvy before attempting this. If you remove too much material from the wrong areas, you can compromise the integrity of the grip frame. Believe me, you don't want it cracking on you.

It's worth noting, too, that most current models come with interchangeable portions of the grip, making it easy to make the grip slightly larger or smaller until it fits your hand well.

Metal-framed guns are both easier and hard-er to modify. Changing out the grip panels is fast and simple, and allows the shooter to create a more or less aggressive grip texture. Personally, I like a very ag-gressive grip on .45 Auto

While it's not customizing in the sense of taking a wood burner and stippling the grip of your Glock, most of today's polymer frame pistols come with interchangeable grip inserts that allow owners to pick something that feels right.

1911s—yes, such grips will tear up your hand if put through a three-day class at Gunsite, but in the desperate seconds of a life or death encounter that aggressive texture can make a difference in a helpful way.

However, if you want to change the shape of the actual frame itself, you'd better be really good with tools and finishes, and have a dash of engineer in your blood. Better yet, just hire a good gunsmith to make the changes, which ensures that the work will be done properly and without weakening areas key to maintaining the strength of the firearm. Note that I write "good" gunsmith.

Another mod that I use frequently is to replace the grip panels of metal-frame guns with a Master Series Crimson Trace laser grip. I like the Master Series grips because the panel is G10 (a super-durable material of compressed canvass impregnated with epoxy) rather than plastic, but in all honesty I've got to say that I've never seen a plastic Crimson Trace grip fail.

Such grips don't add shootability or better feel, but in low light they add the advantage of being able to see exactly where your bullet will impact. You don't need sights, or even to shoot with the gun in sighting position. Shoot from the hip, under barriers, whatever. As long as you can see the target, and your gun has an unobstructed path to it, you'll see that lovely red dot dancing on the bad guy's hoody. And installing such grips is as simple as a modification can be: just unscrew the current grips, and follow instructions to properly install the batteries and mount the laser grips.

I'll also replace grip panels on compact 1911-type handguns with a quality slim grip— basically just a slenderized version of the standard grip, made out of a quality material. It's amazing what a sixteenth of an inch off of each grip panel makes. The result is both easier to conceal and—to me—feels better in my hand.

On a different note, many owners of AR-15 rifles like to replace the vertical pistol grip. It's easy—just unscrew the mounting screw through the base of the grip, take it off, being careful not to lose the safety detent and spring contained under the grip, and install the new one. Many manufacturers make great aftermarket grips; particular favorites of mine are Magpul, Hogue, and Ergo-grips. But in reality, the military standard A2 grip works really well, and there's no need to change it for practical purposes. Aesthetics, feel, or whatnot, sure, but don't think you've got to for performance's sake.

TRIGGER WORK

Changing the quality of your trigger feel is a modification that can be both the riskiest and the most beneficial to your ability to shoot your firearm well.

It's risky because when you go in and modify or change parts, you're altering time- and test-proven mechanics and materials. Without getting too wound up about it, let me just say this: use only the best-quality replacement parts, and allow only the best gunsmiths to grind, file, and hone internal parts. This isn't the time to have your 3-gun shooting buddy do the work.

How to find quality parts? Researching what competitive action-shooters use is a good start—they often put thousands of rounds per year through their guns, and they know what breaks and what stands the test. Another good resource is the tech staff at Brownells, which is probably the largest gunsmithing parts and tools supplier in the world. The guys there know their stuff, and won't point you wrong.

Why change or modify a trigger? A good trigger is fairly light (2.5 to four pounds in pull weight) without being too light for safety; will have little or no creep (rearward travel before releasing); will break (release) as crisply as an icicle breaks; and will have minimal overtravel (rearward travel after releasing).

A bad trigger is as uncomfortable to manipulate as your auntie Mildred's overcooked liver 'n onions. Elements that make for a poor trigger are creep (especially creep with a gritty feel); heavy, crunchy pull weight; and large amounts of overtravel.

High-end aftermarket triggers can make a world of difference in how well you shoot. It's one modification well worth doing to any AR-15 rifle with a standard, mil-spec trigger. Shown here are an Alexander Arms AR trigger and a Geissele AR trigger.

Most triggers on high quality firearms can be worked on. Existing parts can be honed smooth, angles can be tweaked slightly, and springs can be exchanged, until they provide an acceptable pull. Aftermarket high-performance parts are also fairly available for most quality firearm trigger groups. Just one more reason to purchase quality—the triggers in cheap guns are often unfixable because they are next to impossible to work on and no quality parts are available.

Now, it's worth knowing that although they can be worked on, and a really savvy smith can morph them into something darn nice, the striker-fire triggers in Glocks, Smith & Wesson M&Ps, and most of their ilk can never quite match the perfectly crisp, delightful triggers that are possible in 1911s and other single-action type semiautos. Simply by virtue of their design, they aren't quite as tunable.

You're better off paying to have it installed if you're not handy with tools, tiny parts, and springs that delight in going airborne.

Double-action revolver triggers can be made almost perfect by a good smith, and usually without replacement parts. The double-action cycle can be made as smooth as Frank Sinatra, and the single-action pull clean and crisp as Grace Kelly. If you don't know who they are, you don't deserve to own a revolver.

As far as rifles go, the solution is usually simple but a little expensive. Though a good 'smith can tune many existing rifle triggers pretty well, in many cases you're best off to just fork over the money for a top-quality precision aftermarket trigger group and install it, or have it installed if you're not handy with tools, tiny parts, and springs that delight in going airborne.

Such aftermarket trigger groups usually run between $125 and $250, and can come either as loose—but already tuned—parts, or in cassette form, wherein you simply remove all the old parts and drop in the completely assembled new trigger group.

I've used triggers by Jewell, Timney, MCM, Geissele (guys-lee), Rock River, and a few others. All those mentioned make fantastic triggers. Do a little research and pick one. You won't go wrong.

SIGHTS

The most common sight change I'm aware of is the installation of Night Sights, which incorporate tiny capsules of tritium or similar light-emitting elements, on handguns. Such sights make aiming in darkness possible.

Some experts argue that night sights are unnecessary—if you can't see your sights, you can't honestly identify your target. Folks that are willing to shoot at unidentified figures in the dark run the risk of shooting old uncle Rowland as he bumbles around full of Scotland's finest single-malt, or a kid, or some other entirely innocent "intruder."

It's an argument that has some validity, but personally, I still like to have night sights on my personal protection firearms. I also like to have a powerful light mounted on the firearm or in my hand, which assists with the identity issue; when equipped with both a light and night sights, you're more versatile than with only one or the other.

Fiber-optic sights—especially fiber-optic front sights—have become popular in recent years. Having a big, colorful, glowing dot astride the end of your gun makes fast aiming easier. However, they also break easily. My only caution is this: if you purchase fiber-optic aftermarket sights for your personal protection sidearm, make sure that they remain usable for you if the fiber breaks.

A modification popular with Glock shooters is the replacement of the plastic factory sights with those made of metal. Is it necessary? Of course not—the myriad of police officers around the world making good use of the factory sights tells us that. That said, though I've personally never had Glock's plastic sights go down on me, I know a fellow that has. If you want the peace of mind of knowing that your sights are absolutely as durable as they can possibly be, put metal on them. If, on the other hand, you're a practical sort willing to count on proven factory gear, don't worry about the plastic sights—in all probability they'll serve you just fine.

Front sights with fiber-optic inserts are great for fast, accurate shooting. Many competitive shooters have gone to using them. Fibers can break, yes, but in a pinch you can still shoot just fine with the skeleton front sight.

While detractors argue that night sights aren't necessary—if you can't see well enough to identify your target you have no business shooting—most folks serious about personal protection like to have them on their guns. Quality sights with tiny vials of radioactive tritium (safe levels) glow in the dark; adding such sights is possibly the most common modification made to handguns.

Glock pistols come standard with plastic sights, and although thousands of police officers are perfectly happy with them—indicating that they work just fine for most purposes—many folks prefer to install more robust metal sights such as these night sights from Trijicon.

Rifle sights are a different ball game. Most fighting carbines—aside from AR-15s—come with iron sights, and for the most part they are well-thought-out, proven combat sights. Lots of ARs also come with back-up iron sights, but since they are so easily installed and removed, many manufacturers tend to leave them off, saving themselves and the shooter a few bucks and leaving the choice of sights up to the ultimate owner.

In the case of AR-15s without sights—or with sights that you don't care for—simply shop around and find a top-quality set that you like, and bolt them on. Most manufacturers make a series of variations, one of which should appeal to you.

If your AR rifle is equipped with a fixed A2 military-type front sight, your options are limited to changing the sight post to one with a tritium insert to enhance visibility at night, and to changing your rear sight to something you really like. That is, unless you're willing to drive out the retaining pin, knock the A2 sight/gas block assembly off the front of the barrel, and replace it with a gas block sporting a rail on top, which allows you to bolt on whatever folding front sight you want.

Supporters of both systems have valid points: Those who like A2 sights have a legitimate claim that they are about the most durable front sight you can possibly have on your AR. Those who prefer a folding sight maintain that their irons are only a backup system, and the ability to fold them down enhances their field of view. Personally, I have and own rifles set up both ways, and like both systems. The choice is yours.

When shopping for a sight, again, the best guidance I can give you is to go with high-end, proven manufacturers. Good stuff is costly—you could buy Grandma a fine new hat for the Kentucky Derby for less than most good sights will set you back—but then, so is your life costly.

STOCKS AND FORENDS

Stocks come in as many shapes and sizes as do humans, as well as variations such as fixed stocks, folding stocks, and telescoping stocks. Generally speaking, fixed stocks are the most comfortable but least concealable; folding stocks the least comfortable and most concealable, and telescoping stocks such as those so popular on M4-type AR-15s fall somewhere in between.

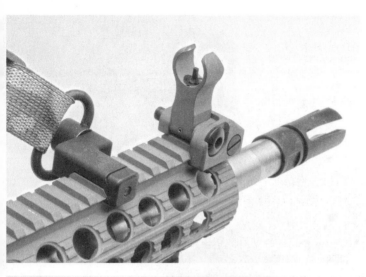

Most AR-15 owners today put an optic on their rifle, but still want back up iron sights (BUIS). Low-profile folding sights can be mounted fore and aft and work beautifully if your optic goes down.

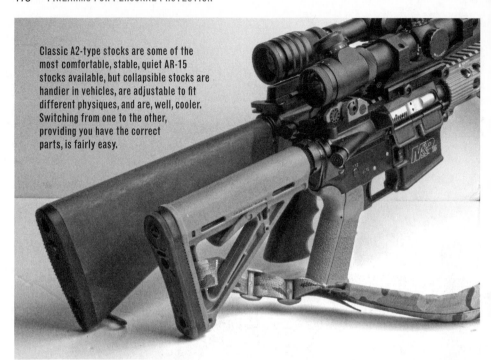

Classic A2-type stocks are some of the most comfortable, stable, quiet AR-15 stocks available, but collapsible stocks are handier in vehicles, are adjustable to fit different physiques, and are, well, cooler. Switching from one to the other, providing you have the correct parts, is fairly easy.

Regarding semiautos, if you have a vintage AK-47, SKS, or the like, I'd suggest just leaving it alone and learning to use it as it is. Original condition/configuration guns gain in value much faster than modified ones. If, on the other hand, you've got an AK built out of parts, or an AR-15, by all means, pick a stock that you like, with characteristics that will benefit your intended use of the gun, and install it.

Personally, on AR-15 carbines, I like collapsible stocks. Such a stock makes the gun versatile and easy for shooters of all heights to shoot, makes it easier to transport, and makes it easier to conceal if need be. However, on rifle-length AR-15s meant for accuracy, fixed stocks make for a better, more comfortable cheek weld and more consistent shooting.

Fixed stocks are quieter, too—a consideration worth noting.

AKs with folding stocks are popular, and for good reason. A short AK is a powerful, effective weapon with 200-plus yard capability, and it will fit under a jacket. Now, that's more important in a decaying civilization than it ever will be in a personal

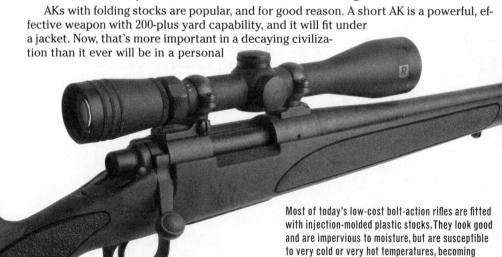

Most of today's low-cost bolt-action rifles are fitted with injection-molded plastic stocks. They look good and are impervious to moisture, but are susceptible to very cold or very hot temperatures, becoming brittle in cold, soft and flexible in heat.

Precision rifles are best served with a high-end composite stock of fiberglass, Kevlar, Graphite, Carbon Fiber, or some combination. Yes, they're expensive, but they are also incredibly strong, consistent, and impervious to moisture and temperature extremes.

If you can't afford a quality composite stock for your precision rifle, a good laminate wood stock makes a good second choice. Laminate shrugs off wide swings in temperature and moisture much like a good composite stock does.

protection scenario in today's world; take it for what it's worth. AKs with fixed stocks are usually much more comfortable to shoot, as well as easier to shoot accurately.

Several companies make aftermarket parts for SKS rifles, Mosin Nagant rifles, and similar surplus rifles. Good ones can cost more than the original price of the rifle, and I'm not sure that they really make the gun more usable. If you have a rifle in this category and want something different, do your research well and pay the price for a good stock. Cheap stocks don't cost much for good reason: most of them aren't worth much. Your rifle will likely handle and shoot better with the original stock than with a cheap replacement.

As far as modern bolt-action rifles go, the very best stocks are "hand laid" of fiberglass, Kevlar, Aramid fibers, graphite, or some similar material, and range from about $250 up to $600. Unlike wood stocks, these are not susceptible to moisture, and will not change point of impact in very wet conditions or break down under continued moisture. And unlike injection-molded stocks (far and away the most common synthetic stocks on current bolt-action rifles; they can be identified by the molding seam that runs all the way around the length of the stock) they are not temperature sensitive, and will not get soft and lose integrity in extreme heat or get brittle and shatter in extreme cold.

Hand laid composite stocks are made one of two ways: with a machined aluminum bedding block that allegedly—and usually—fits the action model it was intended for per-

Most basic AR-15s will benefit by switching out the standard two-piece plastic handguard (left) for a free-float version. At center is a very lightweight Alexander Arms carbon-fiber handguard, at right Troy's superb Alpha Rail of machined aircraft-grade aluminum.

fectly; and without any block. Those without a bedding block are meant to be pillar and glass bedded, a process in which aluminum pillars are installed in the stock between the action and bottom metal, and the assembly is bedded into a compound that takes a perfect imprint of your particular action's footprint. Accuracy aficionados argue that the latter method, though far more time consuming, is the better of the two. For practical purposes, both work extremely well.

For popular models such as Remington's Model 700, a vast variety of stock types is available, from slender, light mountain rifle stocks through very heavy, configurable (adjustable stock, cheek piece, and so on) stocks. Take your pick.

If you want a stock that has neither the susceptibility to moisture of wood or the temperature sensitivity of injection-molded plastic, but can't afford a really good hand laid composite stock, laminated wood stocks offer a very good, affordable option. They're tough, albeit a bit heavy. Glass bedding is required.

Forends are likewise vast in variety, at least where AR-15s are concerned. Long ones, short ones, fat and slim ones, plastic ones and machined aluminum ones... the list goes on. For practical purposes, get a one-piece, free-floated handguard (as AR-15 forends are known) with a rail on top. The rail can be machined integral to the handguard, or can be a screw-on section. It's critical to mounting a back-up iron front sight if your rifle doesn't have an A2-type permanent sight mounted on the gas block. I also like a section of rail on the side or bottom for mounting a sling. Some handguards are milled with a quick-detach swivel stud hole, which is even better, allowing the rifle to ride just a bit closer to the body.

Quad rail handguards were extremely popular for many years, and are still preferred by the military because you can mount so many accessories to the rails. However, they are bulky and hard on the support hand. Slender round handguards with a bit of texture and a couple of accessory rails that can be mounted wherever the shooter wishes are gaining tremendously in popularity and, to my mind, make a better choice. They feel far better in the support hand and rest better over a daypack or other gear. One of my favorites is the Troy Alpha Rail, though there are many good ones. Like many 3-gun shooters, I like to use the longest version available, mounted over a low-profile gas block, and put a folding front sight at the forward end. That gains me a bit of sight radius and offers plenty of room for the support hand and a light, laser or whatnot.

CHAPTER 16:

LIGHTS, LASERS, AND OTHER GIZMOS

No gadget or gizmo can magically make you a better shooter. Sure, some can be used as training aids, but in reality few are. Rather, optimistic gun owners—I hesitate to call them "shooters"—use them to purchase confidence. It's human nature to feel like more sophisticated equipment will make us more capable. But it doesn't usually work that way.

Competency with one's personal protection firearm can only be earned the hard way. It can't be bought, and doodads can't compensate for the lack of it.

With that point made, understood, and out of the way, let me say this: there is some accessory-type equipment that can absolutely increase your ability to defend hearth and home against invasion, whether from the neighborhood pervert or a hostile foreign invasion. Most folks interested in gun gizmos go way overboard and end up with far more than is practical. Really useful accessories for your handgun, shotgun, or rifle can be summed up in two words: lights and lasers. Sure, there are some other handy bits and

If you can afford only one accessory, go with a light—a very, very good light powerful enough to make a threat's eyes water.

Over-accessorizing is human nature. Don't hang a bunch of garbage off of your carbine—it just makes it heavy and less maneuverable.

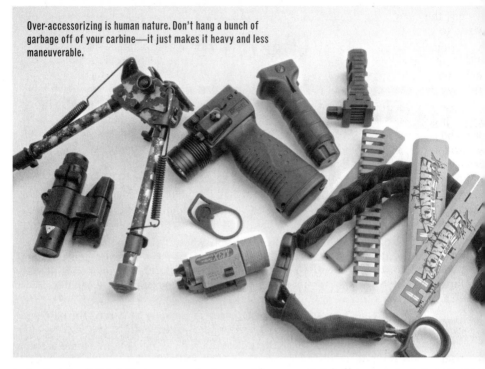

bobs, but don't think that you need a bayonet for your pistol. (As a conversation starter pistol bayonets are great, but don't charge a ballistic gel block with one and expect good results. I know—I've tried it.)

LIGHTS

If you can afford (or want) only one accessory, go with a light. Not any light: a very, very good light. Ideally one that can be used both hand-held or mounted to your firearm, can take abuse that would make a wheelbarrow cower, can be used as a bludgeoning tool if necessary, and finally, is powerful enough to make a bad guy's eyes water at 30 yards.

Many companies produce lights that allegedly meet such criteria, but when purchasing it's best to stick with proven models from proven producers. While I like and use lights from several makers, I'm just going to keep this simple and say I rely on SureFire equipment the most. SureFire is a leader—one could almost say *the* leader— in tactical lights. In combat use with police departments across the nation and military units around the world, Sure-Fire's lights are as proven as they come. They're ergonomic, simple, and tough enough to literally take a bullet and often continue functioning.

When shopping for a tactical light, whether hand-held or weapon-mounted, buy quality. Surefire's X300 light and X400 light/laser units are among the best.

Yes, they cost, but as the cliché but very applicable saying goes, what's your life worth to you?

Various models are appropriate for use in different ways on handguns, shotguns, and rifles, but the model I use the most—across the spectrum—is the SureFire X400. A light and laser combo unit, it mounts easily and quickly, activation is simple and intuitive, and it's powerful.

I also use a SureFire X300 extensively; in fact one accompanies my Glock 17 everywhere it goes. My favorite travel gun (lightweight, holds lots of ammo, is tougher than dirt, and is not so valuable that if I lose it I'll be heartbroken), the Glock comes out of my waistband or travel bag and goes onto the nightstand or tent floor next to my sleeping bag—with the X300 light mounted on it. The X300 is just a little sleeker than the X400, and provides all the illumination I need.

My X400 typically stays on my bedside AR-15. With the laser regulated to point of impact at 100 yards, I can make low-light hits without illumination assistance from spitting distance clear out to 200 yards if called upon to do so, and the LED-powered function of the X400 enables me to clearly identify targets out quite a ways.

If you find a light you like, by all means go with it—with one caveat: don't let price sway you. Good lights cost for darn good reason: it's expensive to build a small electronic that produces hundreds of blinding lumens of light and can take almost anything that nature and human ignorance can throw at it.

LASERS

Lasers are a little different cat. I like lasers that mount permanently to your gun, for the simple reason that making pinpoint hits with one requires that it be regulated to your gun's point of impact with pinpoint perfection. Most quick-detach lasers don't return to zero reliably. That said, some do pretty well, and the on/off versatility has appeal too.

For handguns, the leading company is Crimson Trace. It's been manufacturing premium units that replace grip panels or fix permanently beneath the trigger guard for decades, and CT products have a proven, undeniably good track record. I've used CT grips on 1911s for many years, and never had an issue with a single one. Currently my favorite versions come from the CT Master Series made of G10 material. An incredibly durable material made of compressed canvas impregnated with epoxy, the G10 provides a stable and tough housing for the laser unit. Master Series grips will set you back about $100 more than a standard CT set of polymer grips (and, to be perfectly candid, the polymer versions are very good), but I just like the extra toughness.

> *We're not commandos, we're not SWAT,*
> *and we're not a one-man army.*

For polymer-frame handguns with a rail on the frame's dustcover below the barrel, I use a SureFire X300 and don't bother with a laser, or sometimes a SureFire X400 light/laser unit. How about for compact polymer-frame guns without a rail? You can opt to get a sleek CT unit that affixes permanently to the front of the trigger guard and bottom of the frame, or just keep a good handheld tactical-grade flashlight handy. Personally, I usually opt for the latter.

How about for shotguns? I personally use a handheld light. There are probably better methods, but I don't think a gun-mounted laser is going to help you much.

A good laser hard-mounted to your rifle can aid fast shot placement under stress.

Crimson Trace has been the leader in handgun lasers for decades. The company's superb Master Series laser grip panels are made of robust G10 material.

Compact polymer-frame guns can sport lasers too. Most mount to the trigger guard.

Rifles can benefit greatly from a properly regulated laser, as long as it's quality enough to maintain its regulation with your long-gun's point of impact through considerable abuse. But frankly, the laser will probably be more useful in an end-of-days scenario than inside the confines of your home. Crimson Trace makes several excellent models of a vertical forend grip that incorporate a laser and light, and if you don't mind the bulk and weight, they'll serve you well. But I like my personal protection guns sleek and unencumbered.

As home and family defenders, we're not likely to be called on to wage a full-scale battle with a crew of trained enemies. We're not commandos, we're not SWAT, and we're not a one-man army. There's nothing more ridiculous than a couch potato (admit it, most of us qualify now and then) flashing his plumber's butt above his Fruit 'o The Loom's as he goes after a bump in the night tactical style, his rifle bristling with enough gear to outfit a small squad of guerilla fighters. Keep it simple, keep it compact, and keep it quality.

SLINGS

This is one accessory that would prove vital during long hours of patrolling your encampment during the zombie siege. If you rarely take your shotgun or rifle out of your home, don't bother with a sling. Slings can actually get in the way if you're not used to them. But if you anticipate carrying your long gun for any length of time, you need a sling.

Shotguns are easy, as long as they have sling swivels. If they don't, call the helpful folks at Brownells and ask them to help you figure out what parts you need in order to install sling swivel studs on your personal model shotgun. The easy part is that most basic rifle slings—such as you can pick up at your local Big 5 or Walmart—work just fine. If you want to carry your shotgun in the ready position, like most tactical guys carry their rifles, you can do that, too.

Rifles get heavy fast. Fit yours with a quality sling. While hardly visible, this two-point version by Viking Tactics is fantastic; quickly adjustable, it keeps the rifle tight and secure to the body. Some shooters prefer single-point slings, which are a little more flexible but allow the rifle to flop around with much less restraint.

*Two-point slings keep your rifle
more stable and compact against
the body, but single-point slings can
be useful for their flexibility.*

While most bolt-action and lever-action rifles are just carried slung over the shoulder in the traditional fashion, most guys (including me) prefer to carry a defensive semiauto carbine slung across their chest, muzzle angled down, stock near the shooting shoulder. A fighting gun can be brought into action incredibly quickly when slung this way.

Most AR-15s and the bulk of AK-47s and similar guns are already equipped—or at least have a foundation for the necessary equipment—to attach a two-point or single-point sling to the side of the firearm. I'm personally a fan of two-point slings, as they keep your rifle more stable and compact against the body, but single-point slings can be useful for their flexibility. Your choice.

There's vast variety in the manner of attaching such slings, so I won't try to address them all. Buy a quality sling (my favorites are from V-Tac and Blue Force Gear), attach it properly, and learn to use it. Struggling with an unfamiliar sling flopping into your way when you really should be focusing on perforating the bad guy is counterproductive.

BIPODS

If you have a specific rifle that you purchased for DMR (Designated Marksman Rifle) type service in apocalyptic times, by all means, put a quality bipod on it. I prefer those intended for use in the prone position. However, if you have a bipod on your in-home personal protection rifle, take it off—quick—before you get ridiculed around the block.

Bipods are useful for one thing: increasing stability for difficult, precise shots at distances way longer than anything that the inside of your home offers, even if you live in a mansion in Beverly Hills. Bipods are also heavy, cumbersome, noisy, and about as awkward as any type of firearm accessory can be. So unless you're engaged in full-scale warfare against an enemy with very small vitals, leave the bipod in the range bag.

On a rifle intended for precision work, by all means fit it with a quality bipod. But don't be foolish enough to put one on your in-home personal protection rifle.

Vertical foregrips can be very useful—and very annoying. Some sport tactical-grade lights and lasers, but the most useful are usually compact versions that don't bulk up your firearm too much. The Viking Tactics Ultralight shown at right is one of the best.

VERTICAL FOREGRIPS

A vertical foregrip attached to the forend or handguard of your personal protection rifle can help you control recoil, assist in stable aiming, and make the rifle more comfortable to hold over extended periods of time. It can also make your rifle heavier, bulkier, and less able to "peek" around corners or through cracks when playing cat-and-mouse with a sneaky intruder with deadly intentions.

If you feel that the advantages (those outlined above and others) make a vertical foregrip necessary to you, choose one for sleekness and low profile. The best one I've found is by Viking Tactics, but there are several of the stubby, short type that work well. You don't need to get your full hand on the grip; the correct method of grasping a foregrip is usually with your thumb on or over the handguard, your index finger under it, and only the last three fingers on the foregrip.

For all-out fighting in a variety of situations and conditions, the right foregrip has worthy advantages. Courses such as those taught by Kyle Lamb can help you make the most of them. But frankly, for personal and home protection purposes, I don't think they are necessary.

CARTRIDGE HOLDERS

I could lump a bunch of backup ammo-providing devices into this section, but the main ones I want to discuss are those used for attaching extra shotgun shells to a shotgun.

Most of such are mounted either to the side of the action or to the buttstock. Let me just say right off the bat that if your shotgun has a full-length magazine tube, I don't think you should bother with externally mounted cartridge holders. A full-length mag tube

If you want extra ammo on your shotgun, get a robust rack and hang some on the buttstock or the side of the action. Keep your backup ammo base-down in the cartridge holder, so you can pull them out and load into the bottom of your shotgun while keeping it on target and ready to fire.

Whether you carry spare ammo on your shotgun or not, you should have an extended magazine tube on it. The extension on this Remington 870 adds two rounds of capacity.

Practice with your accessories. Become proficient at manipulating lights, slings, and loading backup ammo.

should give you seven or eight rounds on tap, and if you need more than that to clear your home, you'd be better off using the fire extinguisher.

If your shotgun has a standard-length magazine tube, you may want to attach a shotgun shell holder to it. However, I'd first recommend looking into purchasing an extended magazine tube. It's always better to have extra rounds already on tap in the magazine than hanging on the outside of your gun, where they make your weapon more bulky and less ergonomic, and can fall off.

Extended mag tubes can be purchased at most big gun stores, or from suppliers such as Brownells. Unless your shotgun is an obscure, uncommon brand or model, you can probably find an extended tube for it. Most add either two or three rounds in overall capacity, and if your shotgun has a sporter-length barrel, you may find tubes that add considerably more than that. As long as the tube doesn't stick out in front of your muzzle, get the one that adds the most capacity. And again, buy only the best quality. Choosing a $40 model that will *probably* work just fine isn't nearly as good a decision as a $70 model that is tried and true.

When shopping for an external ammo holder, getting quality is just as important. You don't want it cracking, dropping shells, or causing other headaches. Several manufacturers make good units; I prefer those of machined aluminum over the plastic ones. Whatever you choose, make sure it's mounted properly and securely, even if you have to enlist the assistance of a good local gunsmith. And when it's ready to rock and roll, insert your cartridges into the holder upside down, with the base down. That way you can keep your shotgun shouldered and your focus on target while you pull cartridges out from below and thumb them into your magazine.

Finally, if you do mount an external cartridge holder, practice with it. Get used to loading from it without looking. Learn to load positively and smoothly. Under stress, lots of shells get dropped. Only practice can minimize that.

Within your home, you don't need a portable cleaning kit. If you want to carry one while you're out and about, choose a very compact kit, whether it's WWII surplus or a new-made pull-through set.

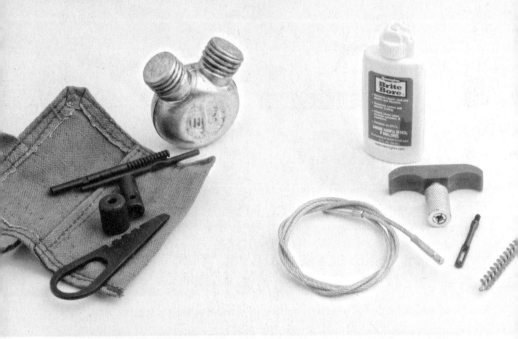

TOOL & CLEANING KITS

Almost as long as battle rifles have been issued to soldiers, a cleaning device has been attached to them somewhere. Early muzzleloaders' ramrods doubled as cleaning rods, and a trap in the buttstock provided a reservoir for jags, oil, and patches. Rifles of WWI and WWII usually had a jointed rod added to the trap in the buttstock, and even the M16 rifles that served in Viet Nam typically had cleaning tackle in their A1 and, later, the A2 buttstocks.

If your rifle with a fixed stock has a trap in it for a cleaning kit, by all means, try to find an appropriate kit and keep it there. However, most of the AR-15 type rifles sold today have collapsible, telescoping stocks, which of course leave no hollow place for a cleaning kit to be housed within. Similarly, owners of folding-stock AK-47-type carbines are left with limited ways to carry a cleaning kit on their gun.

Frankly, for personal protection uses, you don't need one. At all. Keep a good cleaning kit at your home—and use it. With a clean gun to start with, you'll never find yourself in a deadly encounter so protracted, and with such a high round count, that you need to pause and clean your gun to keep it running.

If, on the other hand, you're one of those Americans that believes in being prepared for anything, you can get a compact kit such as is issued to many of our soldiers, made by Otis, preferably, and keep it in your gear bag near your rifle. Or if you have an AR-15, you can find tiny, emergency-only cleaning kits that will fit inside a grip. You may have to change the grip on your gun in order to accommodate the kit.

Better yet, get a compact kit by Otis or similar, keep it with your gear bag, and supplement it with a tiny AR-15 tool and/or parts kit that fits inside an A2 grip, or a Magpul

MIAD grip with various inserts. Several different part and tool kits can be had, holding everything from spare batteries for your weapon light, to a couple of spare cartridges, to an extra firing pin and other critical small parts.

Do I have such a kit on my personal protection carbine? Nope, but then, I've got all the tools I need in my garage. And were I to set up a rifle for apocalyptic times, without a home base for cleaning and repairs, it would probably be an M1A rifle with a cleaning kit in the stock and a few spare parts in my gear bag.

ULTRA-HIGH CAPACITY MAGAZINES

You're not Rambo. Nor do you probably have unlimited resources of ammo. And the local police would not—I repeat not—be happy if you turned loose on an intruder (even one with a very distorted moral character) with a 100-round drum magazine.

Not only do homeowners and self-defense minded folks simply have no need for ultra-high capacity magazines, such magazines usually are not nearly as reliable as standard magazines. Additionally, they're bulky, very heavy, and can have an adverse effect on your manipulation of your firearm. So if you just have to own a drum magazine for your AR-15 or whatever, own it as a novelty and a conversation starter at the range, not as a bonafide tool to fall back on in times of desperation.

Heavy magazines don't move with a gun as well as standard models. Over time, fit can become sloppy.

Even in the case of a decaying civilization, big heavy magazines probably won't be an asset. Now, if you really, absolutely have to have more than 30 rounds on tap for your AR-15, one magazine that works pretty well is SureFire's 60-rounder. I'd steer clear of the company's 100-round version; it's a quite heavy and too long.

Another issue with very heavy magazines is that they don't move with a gun as well as standard models. Every time the gun recoils, their inherent mass causes them to re-sist the acceleration of the firearm, and wear on the magazine well and magazine locking mechanism results. Over time, magazine fit—with all magazines, because the bulk of the wear occurs to the gun—can become sloppy. Cartridge presentation to the feed ramp may become imperfect, resulting in malfunctions.

Can you tell that I'm not a big fan of ultra-high capacity magazines? I'm not a big fan. There.

The only real exception is in handgun magazines. There's absolutely nothing wrong with possessing a few 10-round mags for your 1911, so long as they're of premium quality. And if you want a 33-round magazine for your Glock 9mm, go for it. They're not that heavy, and not so large that you need a wheelbarrow to haul them around with you. But in the final analysis, you'll probably never need those extra bullets. Sure, it would be nice to have them if you do, but strictly speaking, personal and home protection really isn't the time or the place to be laying down mass suppressive fire.

Put in the time to become competent and accurate with your firearm, and place your shots carefully. No matter how enormous its cool factor, no gadget can save your life by its own virtues. Most of the time, gadgets are just accessories, and not very important accessories, to the real lifesaving tool: your firearm.

CHAPTER 17:

AVOIDING CONFLICT

We humans are an interesting lot. Though actually using deadly force should be our last resort—the final step one takes when it becomes unavoidable and necessary in order to preserve life—we focus most of our conflict preparation in priming ourselves to appropriately shoot someone and very little time learning how to avoid or defuse potentially deadly situations.

This is going to be a short chapter, because though the concept is of vital importance, it is simple: When carrying a gun, it is your responsibility to avoid deadly conflict unless absolutely necessary to preserve life and soul.

How? That's harder taught than discussed. Every dangerous situation is different. Maintaining your mental equilibrium is probably both the most essential and most difficult skill to achieve. Without mental equilibrium you'll struggle to read a situation accurately and likely be unable to take the steps necessary to get out of it without allowing it to escalate into a deadly encounter. Unfortunately, there really isn't a way to practice.

Writers much wiser than I have written about assessing and controlling a situation, and searching out and studying their methods is worthwhile. Personally, I take a simple prepare-my-attitude approach, which can be outlined in a few steps.

DON'T BE A HERO

Some situations escalate into deadly encounters almost immediately, and unavoidably. You might walk in on a burglar who immediately throws up a gun and begins hosing lead at you, or you might be jumped and stabbed by someone in an alley. In those cases, get your trusty sidearm into business as quickly and efficiently as possible.

But many times, that burglar will run, or freeze in place; or the trembling alley highwayman threatening you with a stiletto and demanding your wallet or your life may want nothing more than to be away safe with his heroin money. Try to stay calm, prepared to bring your gun into action if needed without being overtly threatening, and work through the situation with—at the risk of sounding like a hippie—low vibes. Keep your voice low and soothing; keep your actions slow and non-threatening, and try to work with the desperate individual. Most likely, you both want to get away with your persons intact, and with care, that's usually possible.

Most of all don't be Sir Galahad. Don't try something crazy. If someone's life or permanent well-being need protecting, kill the crazy sucker that's causing the damage. Otherwise, get through the encounter, accepting a few scuffs and mental scars if necessary, without taking a human life. If, after killing someone, you have to look back and question whether doing so was avoidable, you'll never be able to let go of what happened. That scar will go deep enough to destroy your peace.

RELINQUISH YOUR DIGNITY

Don't get me wrong—I'm all for preserving honor and dignity. Heck, I sometimes wish that dueling wasn't illegal—we'd be a much more polite society if our social actions ac-

Be prepared, but avoid shooting if there's any other way out. Giving a foul-mouthed mugger your wallet will traumatize your child far less than seeing you gun him down.

If you become sure that a threat is going to kill you, by all means kill that threat first. But don't take a life just to save a wad of cash or your brand-new flat-screen TV. Murder is an ugly thing to be tried for in a court of law, not to mention having a possibly unnecessary death on your conscience.

tually had real consequence. But shooting somebody that really doesn't need it neve preserves dignity and honor: it destroys it.

If you're honestly sure that the hooded slimebag screaming obscenities into your fac while your four-year-old little girl cowers beside you is going to kill you, by all means, ki him first. But if you're not sure, don't do it just because he deserves it. I guarantee, you little girl will be far more scarred by watching you haul out your piece and gun somebod down than she will be by all those bad words.

I know, it's never really that easy. The many facets of an escalating situation all con tribute to the decision you must make, and if your gut tells you that you must act or die act. Preferably, before the "die" part starts. But my point is that many of us tend to ge our dander up easily. If you carry a gun, you've got to put that aside and remain cool a a cucumber when the going gets dicey. You hold in your hand the potential to protec life and deal out death: such a responsibility is vast in scope—literally, almost godlike i magnitude—and must be handled with emotional detachment.

CHOOSE LIFE OVER POSSESSIONS

No TV or collection of credit cards—no matter how impressive—is worth more tha a human life. More to the point, where your future mental health is concerned, no TV o credit card is worth the knowledge that you needlessly killed somebody that probabl didn't need to be killed. Unless he tries to hit you over the head with it, let the guy pu loining grandma's silver candlestick get away. Give up your Platinum American Express Walk away from the Ferrari. Alive.

The exception to this suggestion, and all of those peace-loving approaches outline above, is if you're sure beyond a doubt that you're going to be thrown dead in the bat tub after the hoodlums with the cleavers pack all of your stuff into their 10-passenge van. If you can't call 911; if you can't get your family into a small room and cover th door with your sidearm; if you just can't see a way out of getting diced and sliced, the act. Then, it's time to be a hero. Protect your family's dignity, virtue, and that only thin worth killing for: your lives.

CHAPTER 18:

AFTER A SHOOTING

I f you kill someone, you'll almost certainly be prosecuted for murder. It's an ugly word, and whether proven justified or not, it will follow you the rest of your life. How you handle the moments and hours directly after the shooting can be vital to how the following months and years unfold, not to mention how the trial plays out. Because unless it's a very cut-and-dried case of personal defense, there will be a trial. For murder.

How you handle the moments and hours after a shooting can be vital in how the following legal proceedings unfold.

You can build experience handling tough, thinking-required shooting situations by attending self-defense classes and competing in action-type events. You can perfect your draw and presentation by study and practice. You can research and purchase the best equipment and ammunition possible. But you can't buy, research, or practice your way into being a veteran of self-defense killings—or how to handle the aftermath.

Few people have to actually use their sidearm to kill a dangerous attacker—thankfully. Those few can often offer some perspective on handling the aftermath of killing someone out of fear for their lives, but defensive situations are so varied and differ so widely that broad-spectrum understanding usually isn't part of that perspective. And few indeed are the citizens that use a gun in defense of their lives two or more times, meaning that there are almost no veterans of multiple defense-type shootings. So what to expect after a killing—from the shooter's perspective—is pretty tough to anticipate.

On the other hand, there is one group that gets immersed into the aftermath of a killing fairly often. Police detectives eventually get enough experience that they learn to read not only the evidence—the blow-by-blow traces of what occurred—they learn to read the shooter.

After a shooting, every action you take, every move, even the very tone in your voice, paints a picture for a good police officer. So, though there isn't really any way to train—legally and psychologically—for the aftermath of killing someone in protection of life, there are certain steps and protocol worth following to minimize the stress, angst, and potential for being prosecuted for murder.

Who better than a good police officer—one that supports the 2nd Amendment and the right to carry concealed—to explain how best to conduct oneself after killing someone who needed it. I drew on my old friend and one-time coworker Detective Dan Woodward to help me with the following. Read it, ponder it, and try to ingrain the concepts into your psyche against the possibility—however remote—that you may someday have to kill someone.

Every shooting is so different, so individual, that I prefer to think in terms of concepts rather than specific steps or actions. Yes, there are constants (don't greet the responding officers with your gun in your hand), but for the most part I think it's better to prepare to think your way through the important tasks following a shooting than to attempt to follow a checklist.

SAFETY

As the gunsmoke clears and you try to gulp down a flood of adrenaline unlike anything you've ever before experienced, don't let down your guard. The attacker that just hit the ground or ran away bleeding profusely can't be considered a non-threat until the medical examiner pronounces him dead or the police have him in custody.

If he's still present, keep your gun trained on the downed aggressor. Assess the surroundings for additional danger—he may have had a sidekick that watched the whole thing go down through the kitchen screen door, who may take up the fight and try to rescue his partner. Get to your phone and call 911.

Some folks will tell you to remove an attacker's weapons from his reach, but to do so you'd have to get awful close to the guy that just tried to do you serious damage. Yes, if you've put a bullet—or several—into him, he's not likely to be feeling particularly aggressive any more, but you never know. If he's dead, he can't hurt you anymore. If not, perhaps he can respond to vocal commands. Have him disarm himself.

Ideally, have the attacker toss his weapon or weapons well out of reach. If he's somewhat mobile,

Deal with the threat. Then, as soon as you can safely do so, call 911. Stay on your guard.

Whether or not to administer aid after the situation is over is up to you. Doing so may look good on police reports, but if the attacker is still alive, there's always an element of risk. Be very sure that he or an unseen accomplice isn't still a threat.

then have him lay on his stomach, spread-eagled, and press the backs of his hands into the floor. It's pretty tough to spring to your feet or launch an aggressive move from the backs of your hands. Tell him that if you see him turn his hands palm to the floor that you'll consider him to be attacking again, and will react accordingly.

Assuming he's still alive, keep your focus on the bad guy while making sure your family and any other innocent individuals present are safe and ok. Direct them away from the scene, somewhere comfortable and homey if possible.

CALL 911

Get on the phone with a 911 dispatcher, and if possible, stay on the phone until the police arrive. State that you were attacked, and shot the attacker out of fear for your life. Tell the dispatcher where you are located in your home (or parking lot, or wherever) and describe yourself, what you are wearing, etc. If the attacker is still alive, or if you believe him to be, tell the dispatcher, and also tell him or her that you're retaining your gun against further attacks. If the attacker is dead or gone, and you're positive of that, place your gun on the kitchen table or some other easily identifiable place, and tell the dispatcher where it is. Don't clear the chamber or unload it.

Other than that, don't ramble to the dispatcher. Don't try and describe exactly what happened. What they need to know is that you were attacked and fired out of fear for your life.

SECURE THE SCENE

If there are other people present, try and get them away from the scene of the shooting. Be sure that they don't try and clean up, or pick up a dropped weapon. Do your best to keep the scene exactly as it was as the incident came to a close.

As a side note, whatever you do, don't attempt to plant a weapon on the bad guy. It doesn't work. Eventually the detectives will figure it out, and it will make you look awfully guilty. Besides, if you were justified in shooting, the scene will tell the story for you, without any help.

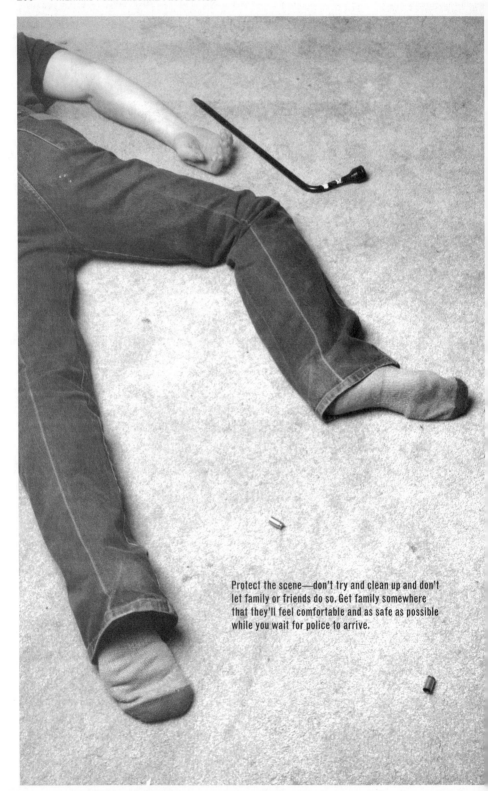

Protect the scene—don't try and clean up and don't let family or friends do so. Get family somewhere that they'll feel comfortable and as safe as possible while you wait for police to arrive.

ADDRESS INJURIES

If you're injured, do what you can to treat yourself until the paramedics arrive. If you've been shot, all of the above might be worthless info—you might be barely able to drag yourself into a different room and sit facing the door, gun dangling, as you try and focus enough to get your cell phone out and call 911.

After assessing and potentially treating any personal injuries, you have the option of attempting to render aid to the guy or guys that you've shot. You are not obligated to in any way, but some experts believe that doing so expresses that you weren't just a trigger-happy fool looking for a chance to kill someone, and probably there's something to that. Certainly rendering aid to someone that tried to kill you only minutes before will look good in court. Besides, it's rather the humane thing to do.

However, I consider attempting to render aid a very risky proposition. Do so only if you are absolutely convinced that the attacker is no longer a potential threat.

PROTECT—BUT DON'T TAMPER WITH—THE EVIDENCE

This goes back to preventing anyone present from attempting to clean or tidy up—a natural impulse after the chaos of a shooting wreaks havoc on your home. Restoring order may help people psychologically, but it won't help the police or your case of self-defense. Don't touch dropped weapons unless it's necessary to secure them to prevent further violence. Don't wander around the scene or close doors or windows that the attacker used to access your home. Don't sweep up debris. It's a matter of common sense—the responding police will want to see just what happened without having to sort out a maze of after-incident impulsive actions. Most importantly, don't adjust any part of the scene to favor your story. It won't work, and will look incriminating.

TALK TO AN ATTORNEY

Usually, unless it's such a clear-cut case of self-defense that there's no reason not to make a statement, you'll want to talk with an attorney before talking with the police.

If you were justified, the truth will speak for itself. If you weren't, you deserve the consequences.

Now, that doesn't mean that you should stubbornly insist, "I want my attorney! I won't say anything without talking to my attorney first." Instead, politely tell the responding officers that you don't feel very well (which is sure to be true) and ask for time to visit with an attorney before making any statement. All that you should state is that you feared for your life.

Now, I've always found it odd when people refer to "their" attorney. Few folks really have an attorney on retainer. However, if you don't have an attorney's phone number—friend, relative, whatever—on your contact list that you can call in case of self-defense, pause right now and obtain one. While it's not necessary to keep an attorney on a month-ly retainer, you should have one picked out that you'll call in case of emergency. And if worst comes to worst, use that number.

TELL THE TRUTH

When it comes to making a statement, of course follow your attorney's advice. It's usually not necessary to get long-winded on the officer taking your statement; they appreciate a succinct, brief report that includes only pertinent details but doesn't exclude anything important. The attorney will help you sort out what is and what isn't important. But don't try and shade the facts. If you were justified, the truth will speak for itself. If you weren't, you deserve the consequences.

Which just goes to emphasize the heavy responsibility that comes with the willingness to use a firearm in self-defense. Be very sure of your target and your target's intentions before pressing that trigger.

SEE A PSYCHIATRIST IF NEEDED

When the immediate drama has settled, see a psychiatrist if you feel uneasy in your mind. Taking a human life—or even just shooting but not killing someone—is a traumatic experience. Don't be a hero. Sometimes, you need a little help understanding and dealing with what's left in your head after such an experience. If you feel disturbed—or if those close to you tell you that you seem disturbed—by all means get some help healing those mental wounds so that they don't leave lasting scars.

If you carry a gun, you should know a good attorney and keep his contact info with you. If something happens, politely tell the responding officers that you'd like to visit with an attorney before making a statement.

CHAPTER 19:

YOUR 2ND AMENDMENT RESPONSIBILITY

Do I believe we—as citizens—will be required by our consciences to rise in rebellion against our government and bleed for liberty?

The 2nd Amendment protects your right to possess personal protection firearms. But it also serves a far more important purpose—it enables you and other citizens of the United States to stand up to the government, should it ever (heaven forbid) become so corrupt that it no longer protects the Constitution, or to stand up against any hostile government successful in invading the homeland.

Fanatical statement? I don't think so. When the Constitution and the 2nd Amendment was penned, the founding fathers and the citizens of the then-new United States had just rallied, fought for, and won their freedom from a government that they considered so corrupt that it was better to die attempting to win freedom than to continue existing under its rule. They knew first-hand the importance of personal firearms—good firearms; firearms as capable as the military's—in waging a death-struggle for liberty, and they were determined to protect it.

Do I believe we—as citizens—will be required by our consciences to rise in rebellion against our government and bleed for liberty? No, I don't. At least, not in our lifetime. What I do believe is that standing in readiness to do so if required can prevent such need—and that readiness is precisely what the 2nd Amendment was written to enable.

If the mental anguish, physical trauma, and soul-scarring of letting blood and seeing the life-blood let of your brothers, fathers, sons, and friends can be prevented by standing ready rather than coasting complacently, I believe that able-bodied citizens of clean character have a responsibility to do so; a moral obligation rooted deep in the soil of the United States made fertile by the blood of those that died to create her.

Clearly that takes the realm of suitable firearms well out of the comfort zone of those intended purely for personal protection. What is most suitable is a personal matter. I'll

According to Thomas Jefferson, "The beauty of the Second Amendment is that it will not be needed until they try to take it."

say this: own a good, full-size handgun in a common caliber, and a good, reliable rifle capable of both feeding your family in hard times and protecting it if necessary in the worst of times. With the two, you're at least relatively well equipped to stand shoulder to shoulder with your neighbors and protect the Constitution that safeguards the blood-won liberty vital to the well-being of your grandchildren and their grandchildren.

The Second Amendment

A well regulated militia being necessary to the security of a free state, the right of the people to keep and bear arms shall not be infringed.

CHAPTER 20:

SPECIAL PREPPER SECTION

Disaster preparedness is in the American people's DNA, and I daresay that it was and is somehow present in enhanced doses in the hardy, independent souls emigrating from the Olde Country. In other words, we may have been selectively breeding for prepper tendencies for centuries.

Whether that fun little premise is true or not doesn't really matter: Fact is, ever since America was settled, we as a people have made a point of being prepared for whatever may come. Most of us have a strong bit of Boy Scout (motto: Be Prepared) in us, and believe not only in our right to defend ourselves against life-threatening danger but also in preparing to do so. You wouldn't be reading this book otherwise, right?

This section is for all you forward-looking folks who want to be prepared for disaster on a countrywide or even global scale. Whether you fear natural disasters such as a super volcano, or a landscape-changing series of earthquakes or violent storms; or you fear the disintegration of civilization due to a worldwide economic collapse; or invasion by hostile government, or heck, the Zombie Apocalypse, the following gun-specific information might just prove helpful. In order, let's take a look at the following topics:

- Choosing a triad: Rifle, shotgun, and handgun
- Quality vs. quantity (cheap guns break, and you can only carry a couple)
- Caliber agreement (with family and friends)
- Ammunition: Suitable types, reloading tools and practices
- Storage: Safe, secure, and yet accessible
- Discretion and common sense

CHOOSING A TRIAD: RIFLE, SHOTGUN, AND HANDGUN

Versatility is important in a decaying civilization. If you have only one firearm, it should be a rifle, preferably a fairly compact, maneuverable one that offers reliability and accuracy as well as enough power to hunt big game. However, you're giving up a lot of lifesaving authority if you limit yourself to only a rifle. Far better, pair that rifle with a handgun and a shotgun. (And though this book is not a technique manual, it goes without saying that training with and becoming proficient with your chosen triad should be a vital part of your survival preparation. It just won't do if the zombies know how to use your guns better than you do.)

Choosing the right models is a very debatable process, and should be determined based on your personal needs and environment. Study the early sections on the various firearm types and work out what will most effectively solve the problems you're likely to face in whatever disaster(s) you fear the most.

Firearms suitable for protecting one's self in the aftermath of a continent-wide disaster have certain characteristics. Be sure you know what best suits your local environmental and social conditions, and always buy quality. Pairing a high-capacity 9mm with a .223-caliber AR-15 makes a lot of sense: both are high capacity designs, ammo in those calibers is light in weight, and the rifle is pretty capable out at 300 or 400 yards in the hands of an accomplished rifleman.

There are a few models of each firearm category that are particularly well suited for such purposes. They are not by any means the only suitable models, or even the most suitable in some scenarios, but they are adaptable and capable and I'm comfortable recommending them. Let's start with rifles.

▪ RIFLES

Rifles appropriate for use in a civilization-wide calamity should be undeniably reliable, accurate and powerful enough to be effective to a fairly good distance—let's say 400 to 500 yards—and chambered in a common caliber. Bonus attributes are high magazine capacity and rapid-fire capability. Here, appearing in order of personal preference, are a few good options:

M14 or M1A (which is the civilian version of the M14). Though this .308-caliber battle rifle had a relatively short combat history, it offers an excellent mix of extraordinary reliability, better-than-acceptable accuracy, and downrange authority. I particularly like the "Scout" rifles with 18-inch barrels currently built by Springfield Armory. Top one with a forward-mounted scout scope in quick-detach mounts, and you've got a beautifully versatile and capable carbine. Drawbacks: rifles and ammo are heavy, and rifles are expensive. Optics are difficult to mount properly.

One of the best possible choices for last-ditch, rest-of-your-life use is Springfield's M1A Scout. It's rugged, powerful, holds 20 rounds of .308 in the magazine, and is notoriously reliable even when neglected.

AR-15. Though this model does require careful attention to keeping it clean, a properly maintained AR-15 is reliable, easy to shoot courtesy of light recoil, and they tend to be accurate. It's easy to mount quality optics on AR-15s, and cartridges are light, enabling owners to carry a lot of rounds. Due to the surge of popularity over the past couple of decades, parts are widely available and working on one is fairly easy for someone who understands the mechanism. Most are also light in weight, which is a big advantage if motorized transportation is unavailable. Drawbacks: the 5.56mm or .223 cartridge the AR-15 shoots is rather light for deer and other big game, and the light projectiles run low on steam past 300 yards or so.

AK-47. Although this statement may earn me some enemies, I don't consider the surplus AK-47 rifles commonly imported to the U.S. to be very good rifles for long-term survival. Many are worn out and don't shoot accurately. Plus, since it's designed for close- to medium-range use, no AK is particularly good past 200 yards or so, and

Today's most popular self-defense rifle is the AR-15, and for good reason: it's quick handling, light recoiling, reliable, and good ones are shockingly accurate.

Made legendary by over a half-century of use in violent conflict around the world, the AK-47 is compact, holds a lot of ammo, and hits hard. Common handicaps are lackadaisical accuracy and poor long-range performance.

past 200 yards is where having an accurate rifle becomes really important. Plus, they are rather difficult to mount an optic on. But all that said, if you plan to carry only a rifle—no handgun or shotgun—the AK-47 is a very good choice providing you spend the money for a high-quality one. Drawbacks: assuming you've got a really good, accurate AK, your biggest disadvantage is going to be lack of precision as distances stretch, and lack of authority on big game (if you've got expanding bullets the 7.62x39mm round that AK's shoot is actually a decent deer killer out to 150 yards or so, but full metal jacketed bullets don't do well at all).

Bolt-action deer rifles, lever-action rifles, M1 Garands, SKSs, Mosin/Nagants, and so on are all useful rifles if you don't have or can't afford one of the above. In an end-of-days scenario, any rifle is a good rifle. But if you can obtain one of the top two on this list, you'll be better prepared.

Finally, in a really drug-out disaster scene, eventually flintlock blackpowder rifles would come back into vogue as ammunition and reloading supplies dwindled. Enterprising folks with a bit of chemistry experience can make crude blackpowder, lead bullets can be cast out of roof flashing and other lead bits, and flints can be knapped. So if you're a long-term believer, it's worth picking a flintlock up and hanging it over the mantle. Right beside your saber and tomahawk.

HANDGUNS

Handguns are the ideal companion to your rifle. They're handy and quick at close range, and are easy to conceal if need be. Those appropriate for last-days use offer reliability, decent accuracy, are common enough that parts could be found, and are chambered in a common caliber. You'll have to decide between a revolver and a semiauto. Revolvers shrug off harsh outdoor conditions and neglect a bit better than semiautos, and those chambered in magnum cartridges are more powerful than almost all semiautos, but they are limited in capacity.

Though it pains me to admit it, lightweight, high-capacity polymer-frame handguns in 9mm are probably the best if you have to go nomadic. When there are no supply lines,

Most suitable for apocalyptic use are full-size handguns with plenty of authority. High-capacity, lightweight 9mm's such as this Smith & Wesson M&P are ideal if you have to "go nomadic." For defending the home ranch, many prefer hard-hitting—but heavier—.45-caliber 1911s.

and you have to carry all your ammo with you, weight and bulk become problematic. I love .45-caliber 1911s dearly, but they and their ammunition are both heavy and bulky.

However, if you are collecting and reloading your empties after shooting—a good plan when you may not be able to get fresh factory ammo—a revolver is a better choice. Spent cases can be ejected from the revolver cylinder into the palm and then dropped into a pocket instead of being flung by the semiauto into the grass or bushes where they need to be searched for.

Without further ado, here are a few models that I'm comfortable recommending:

Glock's G17, G19, and G22 and Smith & Wesson's M&P9, M&P40 and M&P45 full-size are my personal favorites when considering a polymer-frame semiauto for last-day service. They are light in weight and high in capacity, and have been proven reliable and easy to shoot and maintain. Springfield, HK, SIG, Ruger, CZ-USA, and several other companies make good similar models, and if you have one you like and trust, by all means stick with it. Those listed above are what I consider the cream of the polymer-frame crop, but that's just one man's opinion.

A 1911 from any quality manufacturer, as long as it's not one of the low-end budget models, is a good choice. 1911s are fairly complex, and cutting manufacturing costs can lower the quality—and the reliability, accuracy, and shootability—of a 1911 significantly.

When choosing a revolver, one model stands out. Smith & Wesson's Model 686 Plus is a seven-shot stainless gun chambered in .357 Magnum—ideal for last-ditch reliability and longevity.

If you're set on a 1911, take the plunge and buy a high-end model in that $1,000 and up range. If you can swing it, by all means get a true custom-quality pistol from Les Baer, Bill Wilson, Nighthawk Custom, or Ed Brown. You'll never regret it.

Smith & Wesson's .357 Magnum Model 686 Plus is my end-of-days revolver of choice. Ruger and perhaps one or two other makers produce very suitable revolvers, but the 686 Plus is a stainless seven-shot that usually comes from the factory with a good, smooth action and clean, crisp trigger pull. Again, if you've got something else that you like and trust, there's no reason to jump the gun and get a S&W.

As for caliber, keep it simple. In semiautos I recommend—reluctantly—9mm, simply because ammo is light, common, and guns hold a lot of it, followed closely by .45 ACP (my first love), which is also very common and has undoubtable authority on impact. I'm not personally as fond of the .40 S&W because I think it tries to do what both the 9mm and the 45 ACP do and comes up short in both categories, but it's actually a good cartridge in common use. Where revolvers are concerned, guns chambered for .357 Magnum (which of course will also chamber and safely shoot .38 Special ammo) are the most versatile, shooter-friendly option.

■ SHOTGUNS

Shotguns are extremely versatile. Their main drawback is that ammo is rather heavy, but in a survival situation you'll likely find yourself actually using your shotgun more than a rifle or handgun. There's nothing better for knocking over small game for the stewpot or persuading thieving mobs that there are easier pickings elsewhere.

What makes the best choice is both cut-and-dried and debatable, because any reliable shotgun for which you've got ammo is a good choice. That said, I'm going to recommend Remington's 870 pump action in 12 gauge as the most proven, reliable, easy-to-use shotgun choice available. They don't cost much, they are legendary for working through the worst conditions, and parts are everywhere. Myriad versions exist, but I'd just get an "express" model with a standard 3-inch chamber and a 26-inch barrel. I prefer a 28-incher for sporting purposes, and an 18- or 20-inch barrel for home defense, but for all-around use the 26-inch version is hard to beat.

Mossberg, Benelli, Winchester, and others make pump-action shotguns, and many of them are very good. But if you want the short answer, without delving into the many debatable advantages and characteristics of each, go to the gunshop and buy a Remington 870 in 12 gauge.

Any kind of 12-gauge ammo is effective in a fight, but having a versatile selection on hand makes sense. You might have to feed yourself with your scattergun, too.

Need a shotgun? Statistics say choose a Remington 870 pump action: It's the most-trusted fighting shotgun in America. Parts are easy to scrounge, but you'll probably never have to.

Why a 12 gauge rather than a 20? Two reasons: ammo is everywhere, and in dire straits it has more authority than a 20 gauge. Oddly enough, when stores experience a run on ammunition, as happens during every political gun-control push, 12 gauge sells out fast, and becomes almost un-findable, while 20 gauge sits on shelves. Nice in the short term for 20-gauge fans, but the very fact that folks stock up on 12 gauge indicates that there will be reserves in basements and garages across America should the manure hit the fan.

For your own stockpile, I'd suggest getting a bunch of trap/target loads. They work just fine on birds and rabbits up close, and they're cheap. Supplement that with as many boxes of upland bird (as in pheasant) ammo as you can afford, which offers a heavier payload of larger lead pellets (#5 or #6 pellets) driven by a heavier charge of gunpowder. And finally, several boxes of buckshot and slugs can come in pretty handy for certain specialized purposes.

In conclusion, were I personally to choose a single triad of firearms to carry in an urban doomsday scenario, it would probably be an M1A Scout rifle in .308 caliber topped with a low-power scout scope in quick-detach mounts, a Glock G17 9mm semiauto handgun, and a Remington 870 12-gauge shotgun. In a rural scenario, I'd carry the same rig but would possibly switch out the Glock for a Smith & Wesson Model 686 Plus revolver in .357 Magnum. And just possibly, I'd opt for a longer-barreled M1A National Match rifle with a receiver-mounted precision scope.

QUALITY VS. QUANTITY

During my college years I worked in a gunshop. Time and again I'd see people come in looking for a gun "Just for emergencies. Hard times, you know. Something inexpensive that I can just put away and not worry about."

Well I'm here to tell you, folks, inexpensive guns ain't no kind of doomsday equipment. You need firearms that will last, without breaking, through untold amounts of abuse without much maintenance. And the only way to get that kind is to spend adequate amounts of your hard-earned dollars.

I also saw folks make the "Well, for the same amount as this one handgun, I can buy three of these!" mistake. What, do you think you'll carry three handguns while traveling through a burned-out remnant of your favorite neighborhood? And that when one breaks on you, you'll just toss it and quick-draw the next? The truth of the matter is, one high-end handgun will outlast all three of the cheap ones, and be more reliable and accurate to boot. And the argument "Well, I can arm myself and two family members or friends if I buy three inexpensive guns rather than just one costly one," doesn't cut it either. All that means is that eventually all three of those cheap models will probably go belly up, mostly likely leaving you with a broken chunk of plastic and pot metal in your fist and the other two guns nowhere about.

Don't even think about purchasing cheap guns for emergency purposes. That is the single worst firearm-related decision you could make.

This applies to rifles and shotguns, too. Thankfully, pump-action shotguns are inexpensive to manufacture, so good ones can be had for less than $400. But a good AR-15 rifle will set you back more than $1,000, and an M1A rifle half again as much. That's not even counting optics. But if that's the last rifle you'll own, if that's the tool that you're going to use to support life for the rest of your days in an apocalyptic world, that cost is low.

Don't even think about purchasing cheap guns for emergency purposes. That is the single worst firearm-related decision you could make. When spare parts and gunsmiths don't exist, a broken gun is a real problem. Choose your guns like you choose the friends you'd stake your life on—for trustworthiness and capability.

If you're only buying for you, buy only three guns for your grab-and-go kit. One rifle, one shotgun, and one handgun, because if you have to up and leave hearth and home and carve a new life out of a hostile world, you'll only carry one of each, and you'll need good ones. Do your research and buy the very best you possibly can.

If you're shopping for multiple individuals, well, read the next section.

CALIBER AGREEMENT (WITH FAMILY AND FRIENDS)

If you're a lone wolf prepper type, who plans to depend on him or her self alone, don't bother to read the following. However, if you've got like-minded, trustworthy friends, and subscribe to an "all for one and one for all" approach to survival, you'll be well served to coordinate your fighting tools and especially the ammo they accept.

Unfortunately, in the reality of today's world, it's not likely that you and your family and friends will all have the same models. Tastes and budgets differ, let alone the emphasis that various individuals put on fighting tools.

In an ideal prepper world, you and each of your friends would have the same model and caliber rifle, handgun, and shotgun. That way each of you would be familiar with the way that all the guns protecting "the clan" functioned; holsters, magazines, and cleaning gear could be shared, and in case of need you could share ammunition. Plus, over the long haul parts could be cannibalized from broken guns to keep others running.

At the very least, try to coordinate calibers. Get together with your buddies and squabble over whether 9mm, .40 S&W, or .45 ACP is best, but attempt in the end to pick one and agree to all own a handgun in that caliber. Likewise with rifles—even if your bad-times long gun is your deer rifle, see if you can all settle on something common and capable like .30-06 or .308.

Far better is to settle on a triad of firearms (see previous section) and each make a goal to work toward owning the agreed-upon set. And if you really want to perfect your preparations, try to put the same optic on the rifles and settle on a basic type of ammunition to feed your tools. For instance, agree on ammunition shooting 69-grain bullets for your AR-15s, or 165-grain bullets for your M1A rifles. Do the same with your chosen handgun caliber. That way, if you get in a pickle and have to share ammunition, your gun will hit on or pretty close to the point of aim you've established with your own ammo.

Coordinate caliber and bullet weight with like-minded friends, allowing you to share ammo that will likely hit close to point-of-aim with everybody's rifle.

Stocking up on cutting-edge hollow-point self-defense ammo is horribly expensive. In a decaying world, any kind of ammo is better than none. If you can only afford less-expensive FMJ ammo, by all means bulk up on it.

AMMUNITION—SUITABLE TYPES, RELOADING TOOLS AND PRACTICES

Unlike when considering firearms and ammo for current-world personal defense—where high-performance hollow-point purpose-built ammunition is the only way to go—when preparing for a long-term societal meltdown less expensive full metal jacketed (FMJ) ammunition has a place purely for economic reasons.

During WWII, military handguns chambered in 9mm quickly earned a reputation for lack of real stopping power. That was almost entirely due to the FMJ bullets issued by armed forces—with a good expanding bullet the 9mm does a pretty good job. However, premium self-defense ammo with good expanding bullets costs (on average) a dollar or more per round. Stockpiling several hundred rounds of ammunition becomes a frightening prospect, so many folks reasonably decide to keep a little of the good stuff on hand and put away FMJ ammo, which can be had for a whole lot less.

When considered, that presents us with a bit of a conundrum. Assuming that the world is in chaos, any folks that might demand shooting are likely to be very desperate individuals indeed, likely suffering from starvation and/or substance deprivation. Stopping power in your handgun is a good thing. But the way I see it, having FMJ ammo in your gun is a whole bunch better than not having any ammo at all left to put in it, or only a couple of rounds of premium expanding-bullet ammo left in your magazine. So if all you can afford to stockpile is less-expensive FMJ ammo, by all means, do so.

When purchasing bulk ammunition in FMJ (full metal jacket) configuration, consider that here's where the .45 ACP shines over the 9mm: The bigger cartridge's blunt, broad bullet hits much harder than sleek, pointy 9mm FMJs, which tend to pencil through deadly threats without imparting much immediate shock. However, .45 ACP ammo is significantly more expensive than 9mm.

This is one case where carrying a .45 ACP becomes superior to carrying a 9mm, or a .40 S&W for that matter. Virtue of large frontal diameter to begin with, coupled with a rather blunt nose, even FMJ .45 ammo hits very hard. Most 9mm FMJ projectiles, on the other hand, are rather pointed and streamlined. That, combined with the relatively small diameter of 9mm bullets, is what makes for a less-effective stopping cartridge.

Stopping power is one element that .357 Magnum revolver cartridges excel at: most standard ammunition is built with expanding bullets. However, if you're running less-expensive, low-recoiling .38 Special ammo in your revolver, you'll likely buy FMJ or round-nose lead bullets because they're cheap. Great for practice, but not so great on villains threatening life and family.

This is a good point to mention that if coordinating firearms and/or calibers with like-minded family and friends, it's worth comparing the advantages of lightweight, high-capacity polymer handguns in 9mm (if you're going to stockpile FMJ ammo) with the inherent stopping power of 1911s in .45 ACP. Yes, it's another monkey wrench thrown into the decision making process, but only by considering it—and discussing what type of ammunition each individual intends to keep on hand—can you make an informed decision.

As a final note, going with a polymer-frame semiauto in .45 ACP—such as a S&W M&P45—could be a good way to compromise. It's not the choice I made, but it's worth considering.

What did I choose? For around-the-farm packing, a premium 1911 in .45 ACP; in case of going nomadic, a Glock G17 or a S&W M&P9 in 9mm.

Rifle ammunition offers a similar quandary. Owners of AR-15 rifles can usually purchase good FMJ ammo for their 5.56mm/.223 rifles for less than fifty cents per cartridge, while good expanding-bullet ammo usually runs over a dollar a pop. Ammunition for .308

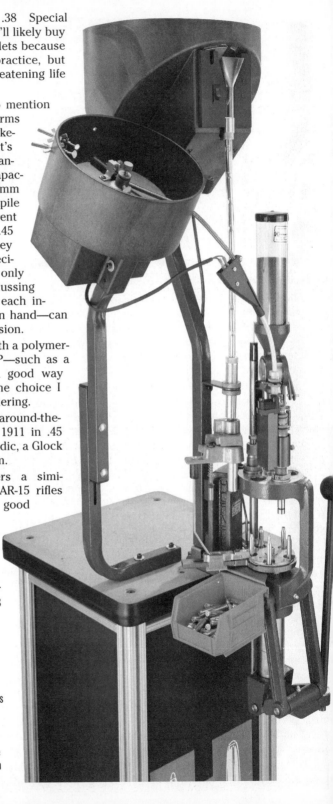

The ability to reload large quantities of ammunition during dire straights is admirable, but the best presses for such are enormous and hard to transport. If you have a cabin in the woods, set it up there rather than in your city penthouse.

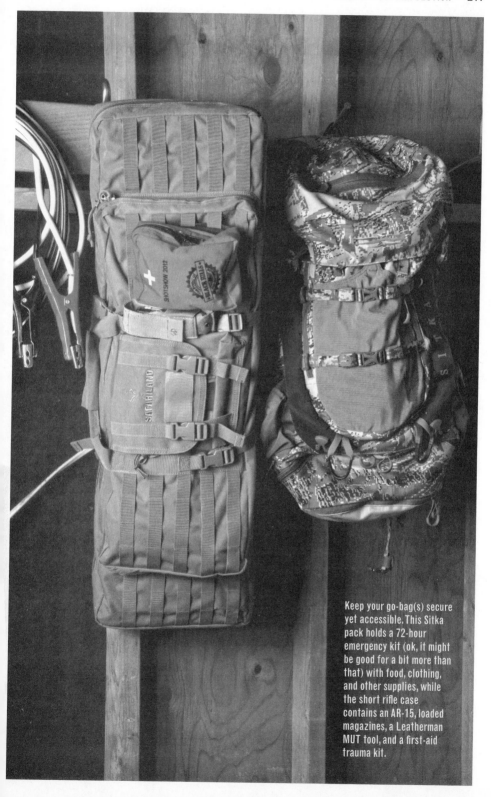

Keep your go-bag(s) secure yet accessible. This Sitka pack holds a 72-hour emergency kit (ok, it might be good for a bit more than that) with food, clothing, and other supplies, while the short rifle case contains an AR-15, loaded magazines, a Leatherman MUT tool, and a first-aid trauma kit.

rifles is even more expensive and is heavier to carry, but the .308 does offer more down-range energy and an inherently bigger frontal diameter.

Aside from those two rifle calibers, most rifle ammunition—such as that for bolt actions or lever guns—is more commonly available with soft-point projectiles designed for hunting. While such ammo doesn't meet the conventions of war, and is not issued to soldiers, it's very effective on hairy bad guys molesting your sister and stealing your chickens.

Reloading can minimize the cost difference between FMJ loads and those featuring good expanding bullets. Sure, expanding component bullets are generally more expensive than FMJ component bullets, but the gap is much narrower. I'd go so far as to say don't even bother to reload FMJ ammo.

As a prepper, should you reload? Absolutely, and via more than one method. Purchase and learn to properly use (that part's critical) a progressive reloading press, which will enable you to produce 300 to 500 rounds per hour, or even more with some of the really sophisticated setups. Now, the obvious drawback of a setup like this is that it's non-portable, so you're best off setting it up in a rural cabin or retreat of some sort if you've got one.

On the other end of the reloading spectrum, get a very compact single-stage hand press such as the Lee Breech Lock Hand Press, along with a skeleton set of the compact tools needed to reload in the field. With a bullet mold, a few pounds of gunpowder, and a brick of primers, you can keep a handgun-caliber firearm running for a lot of years by scrounging lead from building sites, old batteries, and whatnot. Highpowered rifle cartridges use a lot more gunpowder, and to get really good performance you'll need to carry jacketed component bullets too. Setting up a portable support pack for your rifle is a bit more involved, but it can be done.

Personally, I figure that if I'm going to carry rifle powder, primers, and component bullets with me, I'd rather throw out the reloading tools and make up their weight in cartridge cases. Yep, already loaded ammo.

That said, there's one other advantage to carrying a hand press and dies for your chosen calibers with you: If you find abandoned reloading components you can likely cobble together a few rounds of ammunition for your guns.

STORAGE: SAFE, SECURE, AND YET ACCESSIBLE

Every prepper knows that being prepared means being ready to respond—to whatever the emergency—at a moments notice. What's the good of having a triad of carefully selected firearms in place to carry you through half a life of wandering a desolate, violent world if you can't get to them and away with them quickly?

Biometric gun safes and those with electronic locks can—and frequently do—go down. This mechanically locked box by Knox is the only handgun safe that I've never experienced one single issue with. If you've got little children, it's worth keeping one in your nightstand.

If your safe has an electronic lock, keep spare batteries nearby, and practice opening it frequently so you can do so reliably under duress. The same goes for mechanical combination locks.

Sure, you may live on a farm in the middle of nowhere, far from any city, interstate freeway, or NSA complex, where you grow your own food, raise livestock, and heat your home with wood. In that case, you probably won't be picking up and leaving your abode at the first sign of disaster, unless it happens to be a horde of aliens landing in your cornfield. However, most of us aren't fortunate enough to live in such conditions, and most of us anticipate the probable necessity of moving quickly when the scheisse hits the fan.

That accepted, it's necessary to keep your kit handy. However, it's also necessary to be discrete about it and, most of all, safe, especially if you've got children in the house. Few things are more curious than small children, and believe me, no matter how secretive you are with your shooting gear, they know where it is.

So don't try to hide the location from them. Rather, teach them about it as they reach appropriate levels of responsibility, and keep the dangerous stuff securely locked up.

Here we have a conundrum: locked up usually also means slow to access. However, there are a few ways around that, or at least ways to minimize it.

First, I detest trigger locks. I also detest the on-board locking systems available on so many currently built guns. Trigger locks are slow to remove and require a key—a key that you'll surely have misplaced at the worst possible moment. On-board locking systems also require a key that can get lost.

I also mistrust biometric safe locks. Some folks have great luck with them, but I've personally found that they are temperamental about finger condition—dry skin, sweaty skin, scraped skin—as well as environmental conditions. I once moved across the country, and although I packed all of my three biometric handgun safes carefully, when we arrived at our new home and unloaded the truck, not one of them would open. I had to re-program all three.

I've come to prefer safes with mechanical locks. For handguns, my favorite is a Fort Knox, with a set of heavy mechanical buttons that you program. To open, I just twist a mechanical knob to reset all the tumblers inside the lock, then punch in the correct sequence and the safe pops open.

Now, on long-gun safes all the mechanical locks that I've personally encountered are the traditional dial combination type. They are reliable but slow, and they have one big disadvantage: when under extreme stress, remembering the correct sequence of numbers and owning the fine motor skills to dial them into your safe in a hurry is pretty tough.

All that said, there's no justification for stray firearms laying around the house, so keep most of your guns locked up. Bite the bullet and spend the money for a good, heavy safe that offers a little fire protection and is too big to haul off easily. Bolt it down so burglars can't tip it on its side and crowbar it open (a common way to pop a gun safe fast). And make a practice of keeping your important papers, camera, binocular, and other valuable, commonly used gear inside for the simple reason that doing so will force you to open and close the safe on a regular basis, ensuring that you'll be very familiar with the combination.

All that considered, if you feel strongly about keeping your grab and go kit together—guns and all—do so. Just keep them somewhere out of sight and difficult for little children to access (and remember that lots of them are mini mountain climbers). That usually means up high somewhere, so they can't reach. The top shelves of closets work, as do the high ledges designed and built into so many modern homes. Yep, set your favorite shooting tools right up there behind the plants and baseball memorabilia.

Finally, and importantly, there's the subject of ultra-discrete storage. As in buried. Or built into the walls of your home.

If you're the type that wants such ace-in-the-hole hideaways, there are a few right ways and lots of wrong ways to store them. Logically, they won't be the same three as your grab-and-go-nomad triad.

I know folks in the arid Southwest that feel like spraying a firearm down with gun oil and stuffing it into a black plastic garbage bag is adequate moisture protection. It ain't

While you might get lucky and find the gun in perfect condition when you dig it up to show your prepper-minded grandkid 20 years down the road, you might also find a rusted-up piece of once-glorious shooting iron in the rotten, tattered remains of that garbage bag.

You're far better off to purchase and use quality sealable bags built for the purpose. They're rot and tear resistant, and the best of them allow you to vacuum the air out so there's even less likelihood of rust.

Ammo, optics, and small tools can be vacuum-sealed in heavy plastic simply by using a Food-saver.

Storing infrequently used valuable guns and equipment in this manner isn't a bad idea even if you just keep them in your safe—especially if it's in a basement or in humid climes.

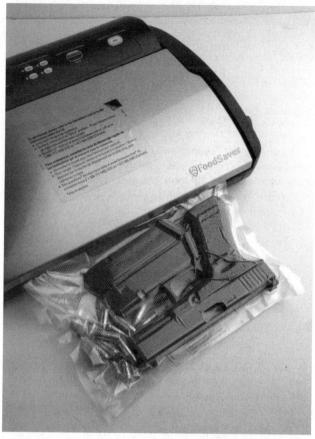

Long-term storage of backup firearms involves aggressive corrosion prevention. One acceptable, cheap method is to spray guns down with oil and vacuum pack them with magazines and ammo.

If you feel it necessary to bury some backup equipment, do it in an area where it's absolutely unlikely to be found; where it can be recovered under cover if possible; where it can be found in the pitch dark without use of a light; and where it will be safe from construction (waterlines, sidewalks, swimming pools—whatever) and agricultural activities (plowing and planting, irrigating). One reasonable method is using a heavy 12-inch PVC pipe long enough to put a rifle in, one end properly capped and well glued, buried vertically with another cap fitted—but not glued—over the top. Equipment can be placed inside; a film of plastic placed over the top to help seal it; the cap thumped securely into place; a sheet of heavy plastic draped over the top to cause moisture to drain around it rather than into it, and the whole buried.

When you place small items in the pipe, be sure you can retrieve them from the bottom. You can tie a loop of stiff string on each and put a long dowel with a wire hook on the end in the pipe to fish them out with, or zip-tie appropriate small bags to the rifle(s) they go with.

Seal off the pipe, cover it with firmly packed dirt, and do a little creative landscaping to disguise its presence. A rock placed atop the pipe cap makes for easy identification and easy access, just make sure you put a few inches between it and the pipe so that if someone picks up the rock to build a fence or fireplace with, it won't leave the pipe exposed like a bone glaring through raw flesh.

DISCRETION & COMMON SENSE

As I've stated, I believe in being prepared. History teaches that every great civilization rises and falls, and surely it will happen to America if we don't respect each other and God.

However, I'm not one to give prepping a priority over living a healthy, normal life. When I was five years old, my father sold our mountainside home to a family that—we found out later—had sold everything to buy a remote place and truckloads of survival supplies. Everyone in the family quit their jobs and came to hunker down in that once-merry house to await The End. Don't know how they had arrived at the conclusion that The End was imminent, but they had—erroneously, of course—and even though I was just a young tyke I watched in disbelief as they did absolutely nothing except sit around and obsess over the coming disasters. As they didn't make payments on the home or pay their taxes, eventually they lost absolutely everything, including the home.

What a tragedy. By being overly paranoid about the calamities to come, they created one of their own.

> *If someone asks what handgun you recommend for survival situations, don't start in about how to build shooting ports into your bunker.*

My personal approach is to prepare for two futures. The first is the current, tangible, somewhat predictable one, and the key to happiness in it is a productive lifestyle that provides optimism and a good environment for my family. That means I pursue a career, earn a living, and provide well; it means I spend time with my family, and enjoy the good in the current world. At the same time I prepare for that less tangible, very unpredictable potential for disaster. What it could be is anybody's guess, so it's not worth getting all wrapped up in predicting one particular scenario and focusing your prepping on that.

Survival, in any such scenario, would be desirable, and since surviving requires the gear you've carefully assembled, you'd better be prepared to defend it, let alone defend your pretty daughter, wife, or sister when lawlessness comes calling. In short, own guns—the right guns—and become proficient with them.

That's the common sense part. The discretion portion of this section is a bit more difficult. Just remember: you're not a prophet, and you're not called to lead folks through the coming apocalypse. Your responsibility is your family—so prepare to take care of them, but for heaven's sake don't compromise those preparations by pushing your opinions and beliefs on folks who don't share them.

Be discrete. Share your prep plans—especially those involving firearms—with only folks that you know well and trust—family is the best. (Even if they think you're a bit crazy, they won't hold it against you.) Harness your enthusiasm and focus it on prepping, not preaching. There's something intense and invigorating about preparing for disaster, and who doesn't like cool survival equipment? So there's no reason you shouldn't have fun with prepping.

If asked for help, give it in small practical doses. If someone asks what handgun you recommend for survival situations, don't start in about how to build shooting ports into your bunker.

Being prepared is admirable, though unfortunately many progressive folks paint prepared Americans as fanatics; as loose cannons dangerous to themselves. I say, as long as common sense is used, prep away. There is nothing but good in the desire to be ready to protect and provide—come hell or high water—for those you love.

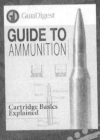

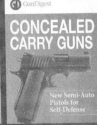